The Commonwealth and the European Union in the 21st Century

What significance does the United Kingdom's membership of the European Union have in global politics? Is the Commonwealth of Nations still relevant for its very diverse member states, ranging from small island states to Australia and India? In contemporary British politics, both organisations have come under fierce criticism, sometimes leading to hasty assessments of historical experiences and current policies. Given the fact that the United Kingdom, Cyprys and Malta are members of both organisations, and that 'Brexit' would have far-ranging consequences much beyond British shores, relations between the EU and the Commonwealth have featured rarely in major debates of international policy.

This edited volume suggests possible – and even desirable – connections between the two organisations by exploring current contacts, fault lines, external critique and outside perspectives. Focusing on soft power, development, humanitarianism and modes of intervention, the authors investigate disputes over international norms and trade patterns. Through global approaches and specific case studies drawn from Asia, Africa and the Caribbean, they demonstrate where opportunities for international cooperation were missed and how useful partnerships might be found. The EU and the Commonwealth are undoubtedly very different organisations but distinctions can provide grounds for meaningful, relevant cooperation. More strategic dialogue between the Commonwealth and the EU, this volume argues, would be a valuable asset for the two international organisations, their member states and their citizens. This book was originally published as a special issue of *The Round Table: The Commonwealth Journal of International Affairs*.

Mélanie Torrent is Senior Lecturer in British and Commonwealth History at Université Paris Diderot, (Laboratoire de recherches sur les cultures anglophones, LARCA, UMR 8225) France.

Virginie Roiron is Senior Lecturer in British and Commonwealth History at the Institut d'Etudes Politiques, (Sociétés, Acteurs, Gouvernement en Europe, SAGE, UMR 7363) Strasbourg, France.

They previously co-edited "Le Commonwealth des Nations en mutation: dècolonisations, globalisation et gouvernance", *Cahiers Charles* V, 49, 2013.

The Commonwealth and the European Union in the 21st Century

Challenges and opportunities in international relations

Edited by
Mélanie Torrent and Virginie Roiron

LONDON AND NEW YORK

First published 2016
by Routledge
2 Park Square, Milton Park, Abingdon, Oxon, OX14 4RN, UK

and by Routledge
711 Third Avenue, New York, NY 10017, USA

Routledge is an imprint of the Taylor & Francis Group, an informa business

Chapters 1–7 and 9–17 © 2016 The Round Table Ltd.
Chapter 8 © 2015 Gordon D Cumming

All rights reserved. No part of this book may be reprinted or reproduced or utilised in any form or by any electronic, mechanical, or other means, now known or hereafter invented, including photocopying and recording, or in any information storage or retrieval system, without permission in writing from the publishers.

Trademark notice: Product or corporate names may be trademarks or registered trademarks, and are used only for identification and explanation without intent to infringe.

British Library Cataloguing in Publication Data
A catalogue record for this book is available from the British Library

ISBN 13: 978-1-138-64791-6

Typeset in TimesNewRomanPS
by diacriTech, Chennai

Publisher's Note
The publisher accepts responsibility for any inconsistencies that may have arisen during the conversion of this book from journal articles to book chapters, namely the possible inclusion of journal terminology.

Disclaimer
Every effort has been made to contact copyright holders for their permission to reprint material in this book. The publishers would be grateful to hear from any copyright holder who is not here acknowledged and will undertake to rectify any errors or omissions in future editions of this book.

Contents

Citation Information   vii
Notes on Contributors   xi

1. Introduction: The Commonwealth and the European Union: Norms, Partnerships, Circulations   1
   Mélanie Torrent and Virginie Roiron

2. *Commune Consensu*: A Soft Power Comparison of the Commonwealth and the European Union   11
   Amelia Hadfield

3. The Commonwealth of Nations and the EU after the 'Global' Crisis: Rethinking Post-2015 'Global' Development?   27
   Timothy M. Shaw

4. The Commonwealth Caribbean and Europe: The End of the Affair?   42
   Peter Clegg

5. International Organisations and the Evolution of Humanitarianism: Cross-perspectives on the Commonwealth and the European Union   54
   Lola Wilhelm

6. The International Humanitarian Regime and its Discontents: India's Challenge   70
   Anne Hammerstad

7. The European Union in Sudan: A Missed Opportunity?   85
   Gordon D. Cumming

Comments and opinion pieces

8. The Commonwealth and Europe   101
   Steve Cutts

CONTENTS

9. CHOGM Returns to Malta: EU and Commonwealth Membership in the Mediterranean 105
Godfrey Baldacchino

10. Back to the Future: The EU and the Commonwealth 107
Carl Wright

11. Singapore and Europe: From Strength to Strength 110
Claire Sanderson

12. Understanding Student Mobility: An Agenda for EU/Commonwealth Discussion 113
John Kirkland

13. Why and How Should the Commonwealth of Nations Engage in the Access and Benefit-sharing Issue 115
Amandine Orsini

Index 119

Citation Information

The chapters in this book were originally published in *The Round Table: The Commonwealth Journal of International Affairs*, volume 104, issue 4 (August 2015). When citing this material, please use the original page numbering for each article, as follows:

Chapter 1
Introduction: The Commonwealth and the European Union: Norms, Partnerships, Circulations
Mélanie Torrent and Virginie Roiron
The Round Table: The Commonwealth Journal of International Affairs, volume 104, issue 4 (August 2015), pp. 379–388

Chapter 2
Commune Consensu: *A Soft Power Comparison of the Commonwealth and the European Union*
Amelia Hadfield
The Round Table: The Commonwealth Journal of International Affairs, volume 104, issue 4 (August 2015), pp. 397–412

Chapter 3
The Commonwealth of Nations and the EU after the 'Global' Crisis: Rethinking Post-2015 'Global' Development?
Timothy M. Shaw
The Round Table: The Commonwealth Journal of International Affairs, volume 104, issue 4 (August 2015), pp. 413–428

Chapter 4
The Commonwealth Caribbean and Europe: The End of the Affair?
Peter Clegg
The Round Table: The Commonwealth Journal of International Affairs, volume 104, issue 4 (August 2015), pp. 429–440

Chapter 5
International Organisations and the Evolution of Humanitarianism: Cross-perspectives on the Commonwealth and the European Union
Lola Wilhelm
The Round Table: The Commonwealth Journal of International Affairs, volume 104, issue 4 (August 2015), pp. 441–456

CITATION INFORMATION

Chapter 6

The International Humanitarian Regime and its Discontents: India's Challenge
Anne Hammerstad
The Round Table: The Commonwealth Journal of International Affairs, volume 104, issue 4 (August 2015), pp. 457–472

Chapter 7

The European Union in Sudan: A Missed Opportunity?
Gordon D. Cumming
The Round Table: The Commonwealth Journal of International Affairs, volume 104, issue 4 (August 2015), pp. 473–488

Chapter 8

The Commonwealth and Europe
Steve Cutts
The Round Table: The Commonwealth Journal of International Affairs, volume 104, issue 4 (August 2015), pp. 489–492

Chapter 9

CHOGM Returns to Malta: EU and Commonwealth Membership in the Mediterranean
Godfrey Baldacchino
The Round Table: The Commonwealth Journal of International Affairs, volume 104, issue 4 (August 2015), pp. 493–494

Chapter 10

Back to the Future: The EU and the Commonwealth
Carl Wright
The Round Table: The Commonwealth Journal of International Affairs, volume 104, issue 4 (August 2015), pp. 495–498

Chapter 11

Singapore and Europe: From Strength to Strength
Claire Sanderson
The Round Table: The Commonwealth Journal of International Affairs, volume 104, issue 4 (August 2015), pp. 499–502

Chapter 12

Understanding Student Mobility: An Agenda for EU/Commonwealth Discussion
John Kirkland
The Round Table: The Commonwealth Journal of International Affairs, volume 104, issue 4 (August 2015), pp. 503–504

CITATION INFORMATION

Chapter 13

Why and How Should the Commonwealth of Nations Engage in the Access and Benefit-sharing Issue
Amandine Orsini
The Round Table: The Commonwealth Journal of International Affairs, volume 104, issue 4 (August 2015), pp. 505–508

For any permission-related enquiries please visit:
http://www.tandfonline.com/page/help/permissions

Notes on Contributors

Godfrey Baldacchino is Professor of Sociology at the University of Malta, Msida, Malta.

Peter Clegg is Senior Lecturer in Politics and International Relations at the University of the West of England, Bristol, UK.

Gordon D. Cumming is a professor in the School of Modern Languages at Cardiff University, Cardiff, UK.

Steve Cutts is Assistant Secretary General of the Office of Central Support Services, Department of Management, United Nations.

Amelia Hadfield is reader in international relations in the School of Psychology, Politics and Sociology at Canterbury Christ Church University, Canterbury, UK.

Anne Hammerstad is honorary Senior Research Fellow at the University of Kent, Canturbury, UK.

John Kirkland is Deputy Secretary General of the Association of Commonwealth Universities, London, UK.

Amandine Orsini is Professor of International Relations at Saint Louis University, Brussels, Belgium.

Virginie Roiron is Senior Lecturer in British and Commonwealth History at the Institut d'Etudes Politiques, (Sociétés, Acteurs, Gouvernement en Europe, SAGE, UMR 7363) Strasbourg, France.

Claire Sanderson is Professor of History at Université de Reims, Reims, France.

Timothy M. Shaw is Professor in international relations in the Department of Conflict Resolution, Human Security, and Global Governance at the University of Massachusetts Boston, Boston, USA.

Mélanie Torrent is Senior Lecturer in British and Commonwealth History at Université Paris Diderot, (Laboratoire de recherches sur les cultures anglophones, LARCA, UMR 8225) France.

Lola Wilhelm is attached to the Graduate Institute of International and Development Studies, Geneva, Switzerland.

Carl Wright is Secretary General of the Commonwealth Local Government Forum, London, UK.

Introduction: The Commonwealth and the European Union: Norms, Partnerships, Circulations

MÉLANIE TORRENT* & VIRGINIE ROIRON**
*Université Paris Diderot, Paris, France
**Institut d'Etudes Politiques, Strasbourg, France

After Edinburgh in 1997 and Malta in 2005, the Commonwealth Heads of Government Meeting (CHOGM) on 27–29 November 2015 will again take place in a European Union (EU) member state.[1] As the debate on a possible United Kingdom exit from the EU unfolds, the relevance of Commonwealth–EU dialogue is likely to gain new importance for all concerned, including the participants in the four key forums now organised alongside the governmental proceedings—People's, Youth, Women's and Business. Back in July 2013, the Royal Commonwealth Society's Conference on 'Europe and the Commonwealth: How can Britain make the most of both worlds?' emphasised two key aspects of EU–Commonwealth relations. First, the United Kingdom, Malta and Cyprus share membership of both organisations but this connection does not translate—at least not obviously and/or not yet—into any sort of meaningful '"link-up" in the EU' (Royal Commonwealth Society, 2013, p. 5), to quote Michael Sippitt, the founder of the Commonwealth Environmental Investment Platform. There is no such thing, concurred Geoff Martin, Advisor to the Commonwealth Secretary-General, as a 'Commonwealth bloc within the EU' (Royal Commonwealth Society, 2013, p. 3). Second, the EU and the Commonwealth are fundamentally different organisations, and ill-informed comparisons can be detrimental to sound political debates on the future both of joint members and of the organisations themselves. In the case of the United Kingdom, as Geoff Martin argued, the question of a stark choice between the EU and the Commonwealth largely comes from misconceptions of these organisations and vague notions of their history, structures, remit and impact, leading to a variety of discourses based on exclusivity and competition (Royal Commonwealth Society, 2013, p. 5; Bennett, 2014).

Contributors to this issue all demonstrate that the EU and the Commonwealth are, indeed, two very different kinds of international organisation. The former is geographically based, with variations (rather than gulfs) in economic development, while the latter spans all continents, bringing together the smallest units of statehood in the world, some of the world's most dynamic emergent economies, and a number of members of the global North. Institutionally, the EU has developed into an increasingly integrated body endowed with law-making powers, while the Commonwealth works by consensus

THE COMMONWEALTH AND THE EUROPEAN UNION IN THE 21ST CENTURY

and has no legally binding processes. The historical and contemporary debates on the United Kingdom's position and policies in both spheres have tended to generate a distorted narrative on the identity of the two organisations, and infused with symbolic meaning and emotive bias rather than pragmatic logic and historical analysis. Too little attention, for instance, has been paid to the evolutions, fluctuations and redefinitions of the European and Commonwealth projects over the years, and to the emergence of the European idea in the United Kingdom in the interwar years (despite notable exceptions, see May, 2001 and Le Dréau, 2012). Debates have also suffered from too narrow a definition of the Commonwealth and the EU, too strict a focus on their institutions and structures, and too marginal an interest in their ideals, policy objectives and final outcomes. This issue does not primarily seek to provide structural comparisons between the EU and the Commonwealth. Rather, it postulates that distinctions provide grounds for meaningful, relevant cooperation between two bodies which share members, spheres of policies and influence, and a number of interests. It therefore seeks to suggest possible—and even desirable—connections by investigating current contacts, fault lines and, most importantly perhaps, the importance of external critique and outside perspectives for the reform and relevant survival of both organisations.

Casting and Recasting Norms in the Post-colonial Era

As Amelia Hadfield, Tim Shaw and Steve Cutts discuss, both the Commonwealth and the European Economic Community (EEC)/European Union have been committed, as international organisations, to a liberal conception of international relations according to which the international system can—and to some extent, has to—be regulated by common institutions, values and principles, beyond the sole interactions or immediate interests of states. In this respect, the Commonwealth and the EU share the same type of principles, listed by Steve Cutts as being, *inter alia*, 'democratic values, free trade, the recognition of the universality of respect for human rights and the role of women in all aspects of governance'. Such values and principles have been placed at the heart of each organisation's relations with its member states, from the first Declaration of Commonwealth principles in 1971 and the Copenhagen Declaration on European identity in 1973. With the end of the Cold War, the transformation of international relations has given renewed opportunity to these two organisations to act as normative powers on the international stage, with the 1991 Harare Declaration (supplemented by the Millbrook Action Programme of 1995), the 2013 Commonwealth Charter, and the 1992 Treaty of the European Union (Articles 6 and 11), followed by the Lisbon Treaty of 2007 (which came into force in 2009). The EU and the Commonwealth have thus both updated their normative agenda, as Amelia Hadfield demonstrates. The EU has strengthened its functional institutionalisation to enhance the promotion of its values and principles, both within the organisation (towards its member states) and outside it (towards its partners); and the Commonwealth has focused on the political dimension of its development agenda, i.e. the promotion of democracy, human rights, good governance and the rule of law as not just a consequence of, but also a condition for, economic development.

At the same time, a somewhat overlooked explanation for their seemingly common normative purposes might also be found in their specific histories, marked by the imperial hegemony of the European continent over the rest of the world which has tended to

THE COMMONWEALTH AND THE EUROPEAN UNION IN THE 21ST CENTURY

shape the values and conceptions of the international system. The Commonwealth itself has been marked by its imperial legacy of institutional practices, common language, working methods and diplomacy. The creation of the EEC/EU is commonly read as an attempt to rewrite the immediate history of Europe in order to build a new unity and prevent further armed conflicts. But the integration of European states into a new common historical narrative did not question the colonial past of a number of EU members or, more specifically, the EU's ambiguous relation to the 'civilising mission' which, along with the need for resources and markets, fuelled European imperial conquests in the 19th century (Nicolaïdis *et al.,* 2014, p. 719). The EU's contemporary international relations can only be understood if the legacy of empire on the societies of Western Europe and on the European construction process is properly assessed. Among historians, research on European and Commonwealth economic and financial cooperation at the end of empire (Schenk, 1996; Kottos, 2015) has brought to light the complex imperial and colonial origins of the European project. The relationship between Europeanisation and decolonisation is the object of intense, stimulating and ongoing scholarly debate (Hansen, 2002; Cairo and Grosfoguel, 2010; Rempe, 2011; Garavini, 2012; Hansen and Jonnson, 2012; Broberg, 2013; Dimier, 2014), particularly in the field of human rights and development policy. Back in 1977, the adoption of a Code of Conduct for European companies operating in South Africa was primarily driven by a need to protect EEC members from international criticism, as demonstrated by internal tensions and the absence of compulsory implementation (Holland, 1998). More recently, the decision to use Article 96 of the Cotonou Agreement against Zimbabwe in 2002 and the renewal of sanctions in February 2012 was read by many in the non-European world as evidence of 'the existence of double standards', 'a response to British interests' and, ultimately, as a counterproductive move in the wider region (Marangoni and Raube, 2014, pp. 482, 484; Laakso *et al.,* 2007). In this issue, Amelia Hadfield provides a conceptual framework for the analysis of normative politics and suggests ways for international organisations to revisit the formulation of policies by the informed critique of both EU and Commonwealth approaches to such questions.

It is perhaps in the area of trade agreements and development policies that the imperial legacies of the EU can best be traced. Current networks have evolved from the negotiations for the Treaty of Rome of 1957, which established privileged commercial relations and shared development aid with the overseas territories of France, Italy and Belgium. As the Yaoundé Conventions of 1963 and 1969 renegotiated multilateral trade and the implementation of the European Development Fund (EDF) with the now independent states, the fundamental principle of reverse preferences remained entrenched, and economic decolonisation a distant prospect (Bitsch and Bossuat, 2005; Migani, 2008; Calandri, 2009; Canterbury, 2010; Whiteman and Adebajo, 2012). The preservation of strategic partnerships with newly independent states emerging in Africa, the Caribbean and the Pacific was key to what was then an economic union seeking national growth for its members and influence on the world markets as well as a way to manage the post-colonial transition and resist US and Soviet competition—both economic and political—in these regions. For all its limitations, the Lomé Convention of 1975 and the establishment of the Group of African, Caribbean and Pacific Countries (the ACP Group) ended reverse preferences and were accompanied by a series of measures to guarantee prices for producers and stabilise exports mechanisms (Clegg, 2002;

3

Cumming, 2013; Migani, 2013)—an achievement in which the Commonwealth played no small part.

With the end of the Cold War, subsequent changes in global trade rules and EU enlargement, preferential trade has been increasingly replaced by the promotion of more contractual trade relations with other economic blocs—and not just on a developed/developing states basis—entailing a more affirmative emphasis on the imposition of values (Nicolaïdis *et al.*, 2014, pp. 738–739). Among partner states, many have interpreted the normative demands attached to the new agreements as new imperialist endeavours. As Vickers (2011) showed recently in Southern Africa, Peter Clegg demonstrates the persistent imbalance both in the trade negotiations *and* in trade patterns between the EU and the Commonwealth Caribbean. In terms of EU–Commonwealth connections, Peter Clegg's conclusions point to two major trends: the overall small role played by the Commonwealth in the negotiations between the EU and the Caribbean, even though Commonwealth member states dominate the region and the Commonwealth itself has become a key champion of small states on the international stage, increasingly in partnership with the Francophonie; and the hesitant role of ACP countries, partly due to a multitude of interests within the group, which scholars have sometimes failed to take into account when discussing EU interlocutors and the EU itself. Tim Shaw's reading of the Commonwealth presence across fast-growing and increasingly active regional organisations also points to an under-used Commonwealth network in the renegotiation of commercial relations in the post-colonial era. As Young and Peterson (2013, p. 514) have said, 'development considerations in the EU's trade policy … have not tempered the EU's offensive negotiating objectives', yet far more can be done to drive the negotiating power of small economies as 'novel players' (Narlikar, 2010). Given the presence of Commonwealth members in both the EU and the ACP Group, the absence of a Commonwealth representation in Brussels remains a striking fact of contemporary multilateral politics. At a time when the Francophonie does have an office in Brussels and when the Commonwealth and the Francophonie staff joint small states offices in New York and Geneva, filling the Brussels void arguably needs serious and urgent consideration.

Setting Norms, Adjusting Policies, Reversing Perspectives

As Peter Clegg and Tim Shaw both argue, institutional partnerships with an economically dominant EU may no longer be relevant for ACP countries for whom China has become a prominent partner, alongside the United States. Recent scholarship has emphasised the need for the EU to give greater attention to external critiques (Orbie, 2009; Lucarelli and Fioramonti, 2010; Carbone, 2013; Fisher Onar and Nicolaïdis, 2013; Chaban and Holland, 2014). In a context in which the EU is no longer just an aid or a development provider but is itself also dependent on the global South's markets for outlets, its political clout, i.e. its power to impose its norms, has diminished. The strategic partnership with India, for instance, is no guarantee of smooth or tangible influence for the EU and its inter-regional diplomacy (Allen, 2013; Kavalski, 2015). The EU's too-often superior attitude to negotiations and its recent indelicate (at best) handling of India–Pakistan relations have given it very little credit among Indian policy-makers (Kavalski, 2015). European Union member states themselves tend to

THE COMMONWEALTH AND THE EUROPEAN UNION IN THE 21ST CENTURY

court new emergent economic markets, turning a blind eye to their democratic or human rights records. In the same way, the emergence of new, less normative models of international relations in the field of development assistance or trade partnerships, like those proposed by China or India for which the state—and the notion of state sovereignty—remain the cornerstone of international relations, have appealed more to the global South than the normative conditions attached to EU or Commonwealth partnerships.

Simultaneously, both the EU and the Commonwealth are faced with the relative failure of the implementation of their own norms and principles among their own members. While the Commonwealth has somewhat failed to uphold its own principles in each of its member states, the EU has been criticised for the democratic deficit of its own functional institutions. Inside (with their members) and outside (with third parties), the Commonwealth and the EU have been confronted with a similar kind of crisis of legitimacy, as normative power is not just a matter of setting norms, but, in the words of Diez and Pace (2007, p. 13), 'will only be a positive force to the extent that others accept it', i.e. as a legitimate actor of international politics (see also Diez, 2013).

Both organisations seem to be caught between the old Westphalian system in which international relations were regulated by states only, and the aspiration to real legitimacy as an actor in international relations, with the need for a functional structure of its own. The idea that functionalism is the way by which peace can be achieved (Nicolaïdis *et al.*, 2014, p. 733) derives from a strong Eurocentric vision which is to be found in the origins of European construction. If the EU has served as a role model for regional organisations, the latter have seldom developed into integrated, supranational structures. In the case of CARICOM (Caribbean Community and Common Market), to cite but one example, tensions between regional integration and state sovereignty, linked to colonisation, the struggle for independence and the failed experience of the Federation of the West Indies, have led to a strictly intergovernmental model of regional cooperation that resorts to functionalism only when deemed necessary for the sake of economic integration (O'Brien, 2011, p. 647). The new ASEAN Charter of 2007 is partly inspired by European integration policies, but is essentially adapted to suit Southeast Asian specificities (Jetschke and Murray, 2012). The supranational model proposed by the EEC/EU as a paragon for regional cooperation has therefore failed to export to countries formerly under European colonial domination. As Hollis has argued, too little attention has been paid to 'the extent to which the diffusion of global norms influences EU development policy' and, more generally, to 'the importance global norms have on the formulation of EU foreign policy' (Hollis, 2014, p. 569). The EU has evolved into a hybrid international and supranational organisation (King, 1999, p. 313), both unable to project real hard power on the international stage (Rosecrance, 1998, p. 15) and longing to act as a true international actor rivalling China and the United States for trade and norms.

Similarly, in the Commonwealth, institutional functionalism is confronted with the organisation's post-colonial history based on the achievement of independence and on the belief that 'respect for sovereignty' and 'equality' are central to peaceful and fair international relations. The Commonwealth is certainly less directly efficient as an actor of international relations (for a variety of reasons, ranging from a small budget to its minimal functional institutions) than the EU. But building on Tim Shaw's reflection on the possibility of a Commonwealth school of international relations, it could be argued that with its multidimensional character (intergovernmental and transnational, South–South and North–South) the Commonwealth might well be better suited to globalised, post-bipolar international relations than other, more formal organisations such as the EU, which tend to replicate the US-dominated model of international relations. With its mixture of intergovernmental relations and functional apparatus, the EU aspires to gain more clout as a super-state, while tending to set aside sub-state relations, both inside and outside its borders—a dimension that has always been central to the Commonwealth. By contrast, the Commonwealth proposes a more informal approach by acting below state level and relying on non-state actors (non-governmental organisations (NGOs), civil society, transnational networks) to develop its soft power capacity and normative agenda, therefore eschewing the difficulties induced by more functionalism.

In 2014, Baert and Shaw were calling for the Commonwealth to be 'a diffuser, not merely a receiver, of ideas', and one through which the non-European world in particular could 'play a truly global role and enrich discussions with new insights' (Baert and Shaw, 2014, p. 1,159). The legitimacy to act as a soft power and normative actor of international relations is examined in two articles through the lens of humanitarian intervention. Lola Wilhelm analyses the evolution of the concept of humanitarian assistance in international organisations, while Anne Hammerstad's study of India's humanitarian policies investigates the extent to which the global South has challenged the centrality of European ways and norms in the international system. Both articles deal with the reluctance of sovereign states to relinquish what constitutes the tenet of their power in the international system, i.e. sovereignty, to supranational organisations, as well as their general suspicion towards multilateralism. Wilhelm's study of Commonwealth approaches to humanitarian assistance highlights that the United Kingdom, more than any other state, had reservations about multilateral humanitarian initiatives, in the Commonwealth as well as in the EEC/EU, as they seemed to restrict the soft power capacity of each individual state and infringe on national prerogatives. This attitude finds an echo in that of today's India, for whom humanitarian assistance has been a way of enhancing its soft power and political influence on the international stage.

Just like the EU in the case of trade partnerships with the ACP, the Commonwealth has redefined its approach to humanitarian assistance in more normative terms. Such examples tend to show that the transformation of historical principles and values into apparently 'non-political' or 'universal' ones, the legitimacy of which is deemed self-evident, might well have damaged, rather than legitimised, the soft power capacity of the Commonwealth and the EU as international organisations in the eyes of their members and partners. The reluctance of an emerging actor like India to link the concept of 'humanitarian assistance' with the more normative idea of 'human rights', as Anne Hammerstad demonstrates, reveals the extent to which the global South has grown suspicious of the normative international politics imposed by the global North.

Mapping Out Areas for Dialogue and Cooperation

The EU does, however, remain a valuable player outside its immediate zone. Some have even argued that its standing in Australia, for instance, has improved in recent years, after a rather negative period when the sense of marginalisation following UK membership combined with UK Eurosceptic influences, and even though the Pacific and Asia

THE COMMONWEALTH AND THE EUROPEAN UNION IN THE 21ST CENTURY

remain Australia's contemporary priority arenas (Murray, 2015). Claire Sanderson argues that in Singapore, the history of Euro-Asian relations has laid the grounds for pragmatic and meaningful cooperation, which includes the former colonial power but also goes much beyond British shores. Over the last few years, the UK government has sought to revive and value the Commonwealth not because of historical ties, but because of the potential it represents in terms of economic and diplomatic opportunities, as a worldwide network of 53 nations around which gravitate myriad state and non-state actors, from NGOs to multinational companies. While the Commonwealth does have value and potential, the redistribution of multilateral relations since the end of the Cold War has given regional groupings, of which the EU is one, new weight in international diplomacy, including commercial diplomacy. This is partly borne out by the wide range of areas coordinated by the new High Representative of the EU's Foreign Policy, Federica Mogherini: neighbourhood and enlargement, trade and development, climate and energy, transport, migration and humanitarian aid. Countries such as Germany, but also Sweden and Norway as highlighted by Anne Hammerstad, have been increasingly present in Commonwealth regions, in both their individual and EU capacity. Far more research into the external relations of the EU's newest member states with the non-European world is also necessary. But overall, inter-regional diplomacy has grown in strength and become a key feature of contemporary international politics.

This is also true in the area of conflict resolution, peace-making and peace-building (Chafer, 2011). Gordon Cumming's article examines the capabilities of the EU as a conflict manager in Africa, showing that the attitudes of host governments, the proximity of the country, the scale of the challenge and historical linkages all influence the conception, implementation and outcomes of Common Security and Defence Policy missions. While military interventions are not part of the attributes of the Commonwealth, capacity building and training, to which EU missions are giving increasing importance, are key Commonwealth policy areas. Here again, EU decision-making and policy-making exhibit high degrees of complexity across national and EU, bilateral and multilateral, intergovernmental and non-governmental components (Chafer and Cumming, 2011). But the trends analysed by Gordon Cumming in the Sudan militate for closer EU–Commonwealth discussions and cooperation in conflict management for at least two reasons: because of their complementary expertise in the wide array of conflict management instruments, including the most low-key ones and the use of good offices; and the historical connections between EU and Commonwealth member states, which are both partners in interventions (through the African Union, for instance) and theatres of operations. While the Sudan is not a Commonwealth member state, South Sudan has voiced an interest in membership and does have historical links with the United Kingdom, making EU–Commonwealth consultations in the region and in conflict management a relevant initiative.

This leads us to three final remarks. First, the EU and the Commonwealth both have distinctive diplomatic networks (Lloyd, 2007; Dimier and McGeever, 2006; Carbone, 2013; Henökl, 2014a, 2014b, 2015; Balfour *et al.*, 2015) that support both their policies and their international image. The emergence of the European External Action Service (EEAS) and the growth of joint diplomatic posts for EU member states, under the impulse of common interests and the pressure of budgetary constraints, strengthen the case for greater EU–Commonwealth dialogue. Second, the EU would greatly benefit from taking a leaf from the Commonwealth book on the principles of a 'People's' organisation—notwithstanding current calls for improving the actual mechanisms of government–civil society relations within the Commonwealth. Cosmopolitan values, highlighted by Anne Hammerstad, find useful conduits in the networks of the People's Commonwealth outlined by Tim Shaw and Godfrey Baldacchino. John Kirkland's call for the Commonwealth and the EU to maximise the humanist agenda of mobility in higher education provides a key area of cooperative work to promote both better skills and better respect and understanding. Access and benefit-sharing, as explained by Amandine Orsini, is another area where consultation and collaboration could have tangible positive consequences. Carl Wright provides insight into the benefits that cross-perspectives and joint initiatives on local government can bring. Finally, as we write these concluding lines, *Survival* is publishing 'Leaving Europe: British Process, Greek Event' in which Erik Jones contrasts Greece's possible exit from the Eurozone, which would be the result of a short crisis, and Britain's exit or distancing, which would be difficult and drawn-out. Whatever the processes, much would definitely be lost. While in Malta in November 2015, the Commonwealth will be rightly preoccupied by the choice of its next Secretary-General, but it should not lose sight of the importance of its EU setting and of the influence this could have on British debates. The opportunities offered by the EU–Commonwealth nexus remain largely untapped, despite punctual partnerships and diffuse circulations. As this issue hopes to demonstrate, more strategic dialogue between the Commonwealth and the EU would be a valuable asset for both international organisations, as well as their member states and their citizens. Malta's CHOGM will, hopefully, give concrete evidence of this.

Note

1. At the time of the 1993 CHOGM in Limassol, Cyprus was not an EU member.

References

Allen, D. (2013) The EU and India: strategic partners, but no strategic partnership, in T. Christiansen, E. Kirchner and P. Murray (Eds), *The Palgrave Handbook of EU–Asia Relations.* Palgrave: Basingstoke, pp. 571–586.

Baert, F. and Shaw, T. M. (2014) Are you willing to be made of nothing? Is Commonwealth reform possible?, *International Affairs*, 90(5), pp. 1143–1160.

Balfour, R., Carta, C. and Raik, K. (Eds) (2015) *The European External Action Service and National Foreign Ministries: Convergence or Divergence?*. Farnham: Ashgate.

Bennett, J. (2014) Britain and the Commonwealth: misperceptions and challenges, in M. Torrent and V. Roiron (Eds), Le Commonwealth des Nations en mutation: décolonisations, globalisation et gouvernance, *Cahiers Charles V*, 49, pp. 233–249.

Bitsch, M.-T. and Bossuat, G. (Eds) (2005) *L'Europe Unie et l'Afrique*. Bruxelles: Bruylant; Paris: LGDJ; Baden-Baden: Nonoms-Verlag.

Broberg, M. (2013) From colonial power to human rights promoter: on the legal regulation of the European Union's relations with the developing countries, *Cambridge Review of International Affairs*, 26(4), pp. 675–687.

Cairo, H. and Grosfoguel, R. (Eds.) (2010) *Descolonizar la Modernidad, Descolonizar Europa: Un Diálogo Europa-América Latina*. Madrid: IEPALA.

Calandri, E. (Ed.) (2009) *Il Primato Sfuggente. L'Europa e l'Intervento per lo Sviluppo 1957–2007*. Milano: Franco Angeli.

Canterbury, D. (2010) *European Bloc Imperialism*. Leiden: Brill.

THE COMMONWEALTH AND THE EUROPEAN UNION IN THE 21ST CENTURY

Chaban, N. and Holland, M. (2014) *Communicating Europe in Times of Crisis: External Perceptions of the European Union*. Basingstoke: Palgrave Macmillan.

Carbone, M. (Ed.) (2013) *The European Union in Africa: Incoherent Policies, Asymmetrical Partnership, Declining Relevance?*. Manchester: Manchester University Press.

Chafer, T. (2011) The AU: a new arena for Anglo-French cooperation in Africa?, *Journal of Modern African Studies*, 49(1), pp. 55–82.

Chafer, T. and Cumming, G. D. (Eds.) (2011) *From Rivalry to Partnership? New Approaches to the Challenges of Africa*. Farnham: Ashgate.

Clegg, P. (2002) *The Caribbean Banana Trade: From Colonialism to Globalisation*. Basingstoke: Palgrave Macmillan.

Cumming, G. D. (2013) The United Kingdom over the Lomé years: a constructive partner in Europe?, in M. Torrent and M. Parsons (Eds), La politique étrangère britannique en Afrique depuis 1957, *Revue Française de Civilisation Britannique*, 18(2), pp. 147–166.

Diez, T. (2013) Normative power as hegemony, *Cooperation and Conflict*, 48(2), pp. 194–210.

Diez, T. and Pace, M. (2007) Normative power Europe and conflict transformation, the Archives of European Integration website, http://aei.pitt.edu/7798/, accessed 10 April 2015.

Dimier, V. (2014) *The Invention of a European Development Aid Bureaucracy. Recycling Empire*. Basingstoke: Palgrave Macmillan.

Dimier, V. and McGeever, M. (2006) Diplomats without a flag: the institutionalization of the delegations of the Commission in African, Caribbean and Pacific countries, *Journal of Common Market Studies*, 44(3), pp. 483–505.

Fisher Onar, N. and Nicolaïdis, K. (2013) The decentring agenda: Europe as a post-colonial power, *Cooperation and Conflict*, 48(2), pp. 283–303.

Garavini, G. (2012) *After Empires: European Integration, Decolonization and the Challenge from the Global South, 1957–1985*. Oxford: Oxford University Press.

Hansen, P. (2002) European integration, European identity, and the colonial connection, *European Journal of Social Theory*, 5(4), pp. 483–498.

Hansen, P. and Jonsson, S. (2012) Imperial origins of European integration and the case of Eurafrica: a reply to Gary Marks—Europe and its empires, *Journal of Common Market Studies*, 50(6), pp. 1028–1041.

Henökl, T. (2014a) The European External Action Service: torn apart between several principles or acting as a smart 'double-agent'?, *Journal of Contemporary European Research*, 10(4), pp. 381–401.

Henökl, T. (2014b) Conceptualizing the European diplomatic space: a framework for analysis of the European External Action Service, *Journal of European Integration*, 36(5), pp. 453–471.

Henökl, T. (2015) How do EU foreign policy-makers decide?, Institutional orientations within the European External Action Service, *West European Politics*, 38(3), pp. 1–30.

Holland, M. (1998) Vices and virtues: Europe's foreign policy and South Africa, 1977–1997, *European Foreign Affairs Review*, 3(2), pp. 215–232.

Hollis, S. (2014) The global construction of EU development policy, *Journal of European Integration*, 36(6), pp. 567–583.

Jones, E. (2015) Leaving Europe: British process, Greek Event, *Survival: Global Politics and Strategy*, 57(3), pp. 79–85.

Jetschke, A. and Murray, P. (2012) Diffusing regional integration: the EU and Southeast Asia, *West European Politics*, 35(1), pp. 174–191.

Kavalski, E. (2015) The EU–India strategic partnership: neither very strategic, nor much of a partnership, *Cambridge Review of International Affairs*, pp. 1–17. doi:10.1080/09557571.2015.1007031

King, T. (1999) Human rights in European foreign policy: success or failure for post-modern diplomacy?, *European Journal of International Law*, 19(2), pp. 313–337.

Kottos, L. (2012) A 'European Commonwealth': Britain, the European League for Economic Cooperation, and European debates on empire, 1947–1957, *Journal of Contemporary European Studies*, 20(4), pp. 497–515.

Laakso, L., Kivimäki, T. and Seppänen, M. (2007) Evolution of coordination and coherence in the application of Article 96 of the Cotonou Partnership Agreement, *Studies in European Development Cooperation Evaluation*, Vol. 6. Amsterdam: Aksant.

THE COMMONWEALTH AND THE EUROPEAN UNION IN THE 21ST CENTURY

Le Dréau, C. (2012) La 'mégère apprivoisée'. Les associations pro-européennes en Grande-Bretagne (1913–2005), in C. Sanderson and M. Torrent (Eds), *La Puissance Britannique en Question. Diplomatie et Politique Étrangère au 20è Siècle* [Challenges to British Power States. Foreign Policy and Diplomacy in the 20th Century]. Brussels: Peter Lang.

Lloyd, L. (2007) *Diplomacy with a Difference. The Commonwealth Office of High Commissioner, 1880–2006.* Leiden and Boston: Martinus Nijhoff.

Lucarelli, S. and Fioramonti, L. (Eds) (2010) *External Perceptions of the European Union as a Global Actor.* Abingdon: Routledge.

Marangoni, A.-C. and Raube, K. (2014) Virtue or vice? The coherence of the EU's external policies, *Journal of European Integration*, 36(5), pp. 473–489.

May, A. (Ed.) (2001) *Britain, the Commonwealth and Europe. The Commonwealth and Britain's Applications to Join the European Communities* Oxford: Oxford University Press.

Migani, G. (2008) *La France et l'Afrique sub-saharienne, 1957–1963: Histoire d'une Décolonisation entre idéaux Eurafricains et Politique de Puissance.* Bruxelles: Peter Lang.

Migani, G. (2013) La Grande-Bretagne, les pays ACP et les négociations pour la Convention de Lomé (1973–1975), in M. Torrent and M. Parsons (Eds), La politique étrangère britannique en Afrique depuis 1957, *Revue Française de Civilisation Britannique*, 18(2), pp. 87–104.

Murray, P. (2015) EU–Australia relations: a strategic partnership in all but name?, *Cambridge Review of International Affairs*. doi:10.1080/09557571.2015.1015487

Narlikar, A. (2010) *New Powers: How to Become One and How to Manage Them.* London: Hurst; New York: Columbia University Press.

Nicolaïdis, K., Vergerio, C., Fisher-Onar, N. and Viehoff, J. (2014) From metropolis to microcosmos: the EU's new standards of civilisation, *Millenium. Journal of International Studies*, 42(3), pp. 718–745.

O'Brien, D. (2011) CARICOM: regional integration in a post-colonial world, *European Law Journal*, 17(5), pp. 640–648.

Orbie, J. (Ed.) (2009) *Europe's Global Role: External Policies of the European Union.* Farnham: Ashgate.

Rempe, M. (2011) Decolonization by Europeanization? The early EEC and the transformation of French–African relations, *KFG The Transformative Power of Europe*, Working Paper 27.

Rosecrance, R. (1998) The European Union, a new type of international actor, in J. Zielonka (Ed.), *Paradoxes of European Foreign Policy.* The Hague: Kluwer Law International, pp. 15–24.

Royal Commonwealth Society (2013) *Europe and the Commonwealth? How Can Britain Make the Most of Both Worlds?.* London: Royal Commonwealth Society.

Schenk, C. (1996) Decolonization and European economic integration: the Free Trade Area negotiations, 1956–58, *The Journal of Imperial and Commonwealth History*, 24(3), pp. 444–463.

Vickers, B. (2011) Between a rock and a hard place: small states in the EU–SADC EPA negotiations, *The Round Table*, 100(413), pp. 183–197.

Whiteman, K. and Adebajo, A. (Eds) (2012) *The EU and Africa: From Eurafrique to Afro-Europa.* London: Hurst.

Young, A. R. and Peterson, J. (2013) 'We care about you, but...': the politics of EU trade policy and development, *Cambridge Review of International Affairs*, 26(3), pp. 497–518.

Commune Consensu: A Soft Power Comparison of the Commonwealth and the European Union

AMELIA HADFIELD
Canterbury Christ Church University, Canterbury, UK

ABSTRACT *The post-war heritage, institutional similarities, and policy motivations shared between commonwealth entities and contemporary international organisations, and their subsequent impact on soft power represents a wealth of unexplored potential. As will be explored in this article, both the Commonwealth of Nations and the European Union represent different facets of contemporary multilateralism, have a markedly different impact on their respective members, and yet are both formidable 'hybrid' actors that can contribute to, and even constitute, global governance, while simultaneously defying easy description. Examining the concept of 'soft power', the structural and normative challenges facing both entities, the manner by which 'house values' are used to define the home institution, and the specific role of development policy, this article offers a series of pragmatic policy reforms that both organisations must perforce undertake if each is to tackle successfully the 21st century challenge of maintaining both structural and substantive integrity.*

Introduction

Comparative analyses of commonwealth structures are rare (Shaw, 2010). International relations (IR) studies, and their various economic and foreign policy subsets, have not fully availed themselves of the research opportunities of investigating the commonalities of these structures, or their contributions to global governance. That there are even fewer comparisons of the Commonwealth with other major international organisations (IOs) is downright puzzling. The critical mass of post-war heritage, institutional similarities and policy motivations shared between commonwealth entities and most contemporary (albeit western) IOs and their subsequent impact on 20th century soft power represents a wealth of unexplored potential. As Shaw argues (2010, p. 333) argues, the various commonwealth entities[1] 'deserve to be juxtaposed with myriad other international networks' with the hope that such 'overdue attention might also generate policy considerations or innovations'. The themes pursued in this special issue are thus both salient and belated. As will be explored in this article, both the Commonwealth of Nations and the European Union (EU) represent different facets of contemporary multilateralism, have a markedly different impact on their respective members, and yet represent 'distinctive global networks' that struggle, with varying degrees of success, to transcend their inheritance (Shaw, 2010, p. 334). This makes them both formidable 'hybrid' actors that can contribute to, and even constitute, global governance, while simultaneously—even maddeningly—defying easy description.

This article begins by examining the concept of 'soft power', and its ability to give meaning to, and emerge from, the normative foundations of entities such as the EU and the Commonwealth. From there, it moves on to survey the structural and normative challenges facing both entities, suggesting that both operate on a value-based foundation, but have dealt differently with contemporary challenges to their respective normative templates. From there, the article examines the specific manner by which 'house values' are used to define the home institution, calibrate its relations to its members, and ultimately influence non-members. Here the role of development policy takes centre stage, with the Commonwealth being repeatedly advised to 'promote positive economic outcomes and prosperity through better enforcing its values', and the EU moving development policy alongside diplomacy and defence as part of its broad spectrum approach to international engagement (Gruenbaum, 2014, p. 370). The article concludes by offering a series of pragmatic policy reforms that both must undertake if each is to tackle successfully the 21st century challenge of maintaining both structural and substantive integrity.

Soft Power: From Moral Agenda to High-minded Foreign Policy

The concept of soft power continues to fascinate both scholars and practitioners of foreign policy. Defining it, locating it on a spectrum, and then identifying decent case studies represent much of the traditional outputs in this area. Case studies illustrating the practicalities of such broad concepts operate best when there are both successful and imperfect examples of a policy's execution, and particularly when well-known demonstrations sit alongside lesser known instances. The EU won the 2012 Nobel Peace Prize for its unwavering commitment in policy, if not always in practice, to ensuring that *norms* remained at the heart of its philosophy, and that *soft power* remained the primary method of transforming both Europe and the European neighbourhood. Yet the EU has singularly failed to implement a range of practical norms at home, most notably financial reform, while its track record on instilling key norms in the new range of post-enlargement partners beyond its borders remains desperately uneven. The Commonwealth has a slightly older track record in terms of identifying working, exportable political norms that could act generically as a template for governance across a richly varied set of members. This should endow the Commonwealth with an established understanding of how key facets of soft power, such as civil society advocacy, private sector regeneration and development funding, can all impart normative change. Yet the Commonwealth, as a body politic, lies uneasy under the burden of carrying and implementing its own norms. The task has transformed it into an 'association of states divided by common values' that undermine its historical aspirations of a common moral agenda (Gruenbaum, 2014, p. 369). Both entities make good soft power case studies, though in different and possibly unexpected ways.

THE COMMONWEALTH AND THE EUROPEAN UNION IN THE 21ST CENTURY

There is a pleasingly interdisciplinary body of work[2] exploring the concept of soft power. Unlike many other concepts in IR (including 'power' itself), soft power provides analysts and policy-makers alike with an abundance of understanding of interpretations of power, diplomacy, state behaviour and foreign policy. Some argue that such conceptual fecundity prevents decent theorising—rendering 'soft power' not 'analytically rigorous enough to improve policy', and whose 'endless hijacking has derailed serious policy discussions, diluting them into sophomoric academic stand-offs' (Khanna, 2012). Equally however, soft power provides new depth to the rudimentary foreign policy spectrum (Hoover Institution Stratford University, 2012).

Introduced by IR theorist Joseph Nye (2004, p. 5), the essence of soft power lies in the ability of a given political entity—a state or non-state actor—to induce other actors and entities in the international system to desire similar goals and outcomes to the initiating actor. Based on the sheer attractiveness of its composition, whether political, economic or cultural, soft power should simply outflank the brute force of hard power, sidestepping rude compulsion and raw coercion through the influence of a wider set of ideas, preferences and behaviours (Joseph Nye, 2004, p. 5). Influencing preferences has a slow, constitutive impact on the substance of the ideas of 'the other', but may also produce a swifter, or at least more visible behavioural impact by way of changed policies (Ferguson, 2003). Soft power attractiveness thus establishes the conditions that subsequently generate a shift of mind-set, rather than a forcible alteration via coercion (Cini and Perez-Solorzano Borragan, 2009, p. 413). The range of what a given actor can demonstrate as attractive (and ultimately emulative) ranges from a transparent political system to sophisticated cultural values, from economic strength and a particular market or currency system, to agreeable foreign policies.[3]

Taken together, the quality of the overall *governing idea* representative of a given actor, and of the ensuing range of *policies* (from foreign and security to domestic) inducing like-mindedness in others, lies at the heart of soft power. When those ideas relate to both the ethics guiding daily human behaviour and the morals guiding broader principles of state interaction they become representative of *codes of conduct* calibrating the interaction of entire societies as either proper or improper. Norms entail power of, and over, ideas; the growth and impact of a given belief system or *idée force* 'starting with the beliefs of the "founding fathers" and extending through its appeal to widely differing political temperaments' (Manners, 2002, p. 239). By instilling foundational, even civilisational values at the heart of a political entity, the spectrum of soft power tools utilised by a given actor widens from merely emulative and practical to virtuous, requisite and necessary. Generally, such values are antithetical to traditional hard power virtues, and revolve around pacific and universal understandings of respect and integrity, leveraged instead via civilian, economic, societal and cultural tools (Wilson, 2008). *Normative power* is added to the *soft power* spectrum; and as it does so, it moves from merely characterising a type of foreign policy to defining the very actor itself. Accordingly, one does not merely possess normative foreign policy tools, one also becomes a normative power.[4]

Is there evidence therefore that both the EU and the Commonwealth represent not only soft power through their use of instruments such as development aid and diplomacy, but also represent a normative, i.e. a value-based, power? Does their respective capacity to achieve both goals for their own members and change within the international system stem primarily from their ability to promulgate their norm-based soft power foreign policies? The short answer is yes, but in very different ways. The longer answer entails a non-exhaustive comparison of the soft power composition of these two organisations, specifically the moral agenda propounded and the development policy promoted, as well as their ability to accommodate challenges from within and among their own members.

Structural and Normative Challenges: The Widening Gyre

Both the EU and the Commonwealth of Nations have dominated the latter part of the 20th century as unique and rather hybrid non-state actors. The EU remains fiendishly difficult to define in terms of its shared 'actorness' (Niemann and Bretherton, 2013), which gathers both sovereign states and supranational institutions, conjoined by unique decision-making methods with a seemingly endless range of polyvalent policies. Its normative power stems from the range of values that emerged during its transition from common market into political union in the early 1990s to define a self-referential European identity, a rigorous set of criteria applied to prospective members and, over time, a strategic culture. European Union soft power is far more institutionalised and developed than that found in the Commonwealth (and possibly any other IO apart from the United Nations (UN)), encapsulating a robust range of diplomatic, political, social, cultural, security and economic tools that it has refined over subsequent treaty iterations. This does not necessarily equate to a clear internal vision or an external identity, at least in the traditional sense. But the union is arguably endowed with, and defined by, its soft power support system. The outcome, as Moravcsik (2010, p. 92) suggests, is that the EU 'specializes in the use of economic influence, international law, "soft power" ... In fact, Europe today is more effective at projecting civilian power globally than any other state or non-state actor'. Manners and others have taken this further in recent years, refining the EU's soft power from a civilian power or trading power to one 'with a focus on normative power of an ideational nature characterized by common principles and a willingness to disregard Westphalian conventions', whose 'ability to shape conceptions of "normal" in international relations' is considerable, fascinatingly polyvalent but still uneven (Manners, 2002, p. 239).

The Commonwealth, meanwhile, is a family of nations gathering together 53 states whose links now transcend their post-colonial heritage and which blends intergovernmental and non-governmental dynamics in a variety of ways. The Commonwealth gathers its normative power from the values enshrined in the Commonwealth Charter, and its soft power from the economic support it provides and the range of official and non-official channels that support public and private sector, governmental and civil society elements across each of its members.

Such comparisons present an interesting, relatively positive view of the two entities. Neither possesses a robust spectrum of traditional foreign policy tools; uniquely, however, both have made normative the virtue of their circumscribed necessities as non-state actors. However, both the EU and the Commonwealth remain targets for all manner of criticism—much of it aimed at their respective inabilities to wield a normative identity with genuine legitimacy or to execute their soft power tools with real effectiveness. A cynical reading of the Commonwealth is all too easy. From within *The Round Table* journal to swathes of publicity and scholarship, the sense gained in the past five years is that the Commonwealth is somehow not fit for purpose. The EU, in its attempts to construct itself as a soft power actor, both regionally and internationally, suffers these same slings and arrows, but has managed to move (albeit glacially) onwards. For both entities, much of the criticism is too blurred or emotive to understand fully what the *source* of the problem is, and how to correct it. Looking closely, however, there are generally three central criticisms specifically attached to the *soft power* quality of the Commonwealth and the EU, and which should remain separate from critiques of irrelevance, obsolescence, desuetude, etc.

First are accusations that either entity has failed *substantively*, i.e. not living up to its ambitiously normative foundations. Here, there is clearly cause for concern. *Pace* Howell (2011, p. 252), and with the possible exception of participation at sporting events, the Commonwealth is patently not an 'extraordinary association of like-minded states'. The Commonwealth has defaulted on defining its own values in a way that systematically connects its foundational documents to the practices of its organs and agencies, and defaulted in defending its values as the primary basis of association among its members. Absent a clear values-base, the *raison d'être* of the Commonwealth remains critically hampered; no amount of 'resilience and adaptability' will produce an outcome other than fatal stultification (Howell, 2011, p. 252). The EU, primarily as a result of enlargements in 2004, 2007 and 2013, emerges arguably better as a normative entrepreneur and exporter. Evidence of the EU's stout commitment to a set of cardinal norms and their translation into an effective east–west foreign policy producing durable post-Soviet transformation was acknowledged in 2012 with the Nobel Peace Prize. North–south engagements with the Mediterranean, however, have proved more sporadic: witness the failure of the EU to get a decent grasp on either its southern 'neighbourhood' or its fractious eastern hinterland.

Second, criticisms exist suggesting that the Commonwealth has defaulted *procedurally*, by failing to provide itself with the correct structures and tools by which to make these still-salient norms effective across its entire membership. Here, the much-vaunted 'quiet diplomacy' of both the Commonwealth and the EU is under scrutiny, and will be examined below on the basis of their respective development policies.

Third, censure as a result of the generic–genetic dilemma bedevils many normative powers in their attempt to represent an overarching value-based entity while attempting to offer tailor-made solutions for key members. Fragmentation appears when the former is not strong enough to transform all members in a top-down manner, and also when the latter fail to produce bottom-up results. As Gruenbaum argued in 2014, the reason that the Commonwealth ironically 'increasingly appears to be an association of states divided by common values' is because common values cut both ways: they represent both 'the Commonwealth as standing for "universal" values' and a recipe by which 'to further the development of their country' in their own way (Gruenbaum, 2014, p. 369). This is a fair comment, and one that can be levelled at both the Commonwealth and the EU, although it should be noted that development as both a philosophy and a policy has changed radically in recent years, and the shift has exacerbated rather than eradicated this bipolar quality.[5]

Development Aid: Broke or Brokerage?

While norms are discussed below, it is the *quantitative effect* of numbers as well as the *qualitative affect* of norms that are equally vital; and in this case, the impact of development policy literally speaks volumes. Development aid, traditionally subsuming both preferential forms of trade and aid (either conditionally or unconditionally applied), and the policies that accompany it, is one of the clearest and most easily distinguishable forms of soft power. The two, however, do not always work easily together. Trade can be managed in largely instrumental methods; but aid comes with the full force of the intentions, desires and designs of the funder firmly attached. As I have argued elsewhere in relation to EU aid, development policy thus possesses 'a set of oppositional, or Janus-like, forces passing through the same gateway. The first force is one of nonreciprocal aid born of the desire to assist the developing world in a financial, largely non-interventionist manner. The second force is assistance that transmits the political values, norms and securitised approaches of the donor in order to influence Third World governance' (Hadfield, 2007, p. 39).

Aid therefore needs to be carefully examined in terms of the underlying rationale of the aid giver, the distributive methodology adhered to, the criteria of conditionality in terms of norms to be established or strengthened, expectations and modes of evaluation measuring the quality and quantity of change brought to bear.

The European Union

A brief look at the development aid statistics of the EU[6] shows that the EU remains favourably disposed towards the need and modes of giving. Despite a fairly draconian overhaul of development funding in light of the 2014 EU budget (European Union, 2013), the EU remains the world leader in terms of overseas development aid generosity. With €55.2 billion of official development assistance, the EU institutions and 28 EU countries together provided for more than half of global official aid, which makes it the biggest donor of development aid in the world. The EU has a global presence in 140 countries—a form of actorness ranging from one of a host of foreign funders (e.g. India) to the most substantial funder in the region (e.g. Palestine). Having begun with a fairly rudimentary structure of aid giving, based first on preferential trade and unconditional aid in the 1970s, the 1980s saw the rise of tempered trade preferences and the increase of given norms underwriting and eventually conditioning the modalities of all EU giving. Categorised as 'Political Dimensions', the EU's own norms were steadily introduced into each of the Country Strategy Papers set out to guide the specific EU–recipient state relations. As such, democracy, human rights and the rule of law were established as 'essential elements', while the ever-ambiguous norm of good governance operated as a 'fundamental element', all with various mechanisms attached to encourage the observance of these norms in pursuance of aid receipt.

What is interesting is the persistently polyvalent nature of the EU's aid philosophy: its inputs generally comprise a complex series of conditional reforms and transformations on the basis of increasingly strictly monitored guidelines, while the outputs of such reforms generally dovetail with other forms of EU actorness in a given country, ranging from the political to the cultural (including a possible security presence), and encompassing specialist EU assistance and expertise on human rights, electoral observation, governance and crisis resolution. Under the aegis of the 3-D approach—a holistic foreign policy blend of development, diplomacy and (if needed) defence—the EU's development activities now rarely take the form of tranches of aid given in stand-alone fashion. From

THE COMMONWEALTH AND THE EUROPEAN UNION IN THE 21ST CENTURY

the perspective of enhancing its own foreign policy, as recently argued by van Reisen (2007, p. 59), 'EU development co-operation has ... been continuously under the pressure of subordination to the EU's Common and Foreign and Security Policy and of being linked to other external priorities'. A more cosmopolitan interpretation might suggest that the EU has rebuffed American attempts at eradicating preferences, and has fought tenaciously for the graduated integration of smaller, poorer states into the global trading network, keeping a generally strong commitment to poverty-eradication and the Millennium Development Goals (moving into their second generation as of 2015).

The EU has—through a series of searing internal audits and external funding embarrassments—learned the hard way (Mold, 2007; Carbone, 2009): cost-efficiency born of recent austerity measures within Brussels, but also the diplomatic economies of scale to be had when layering aid to developing states with related efforts in the fields of humanitarian aid, sustainable development, capacity building, training, and efforts to promote local and regional trade, alongside gradual market-opening. Not everyone is on board, of course. The 2000 Cotonou Agreement between the EU and African, Caribbean and Pacific (ACP) countries, and its two successive iterations, are vaunted by the EU as the most ground-breaking, polyvalent and comprehensive of aid partnerships (Flint, 2008; European Union, 2014). Pioneering to some extent, the EU has moved beyond the initial grouping of ACP states to regional blocs, or Economic Partnership Agreements (EPAs),[7] to encourage regional trade, political dialogue and security burden-sharing. This entails gradual shedding of preferential trade against a backdrop of enhanced normative demands by the EU, and has not been welcomed with open arms by all ACP states (European Union, 2012).

Cotonou, designed to run for a 20-year period, has shifted from a strict focus on poverty-eradication to a broader focus on security and stabilisation, possibly to the detriment of the absolute minimal needs of the poorest of states (Hadfield, 2007). Overall, however, the EU remains a global aid leader. Its philosophy of giving and its practice of disbursement are generally clearly mapped out, and for the most part are visible in terms of impact. The controlling Directorate General of the European Commission, DG DevCo, has amassed, and indeed learned from, decades of experience in leveraging soft power of aid by ensuring that the conditions of giving and the conditions of receiving remain as commensurate as possible for as long as possible. Looking for a magnifying impact of policies that reinforce each other, the EU has gradually learned that coherence within development policy increases 'the impact that other EU policy areas can potentially have on international development' (Hurt, 2010, p. 160). With a growing strategic culture (Meyer, 2006), but without the traditional forms of hard power, the EU's soft power is thus heavily dependent upon its ability to keep its own normative template both visible and exportable, chiefly via development and diplomacy.

The Commonwealth

The Commonwealth is also an historic—if not necessarily a prolific—aid giver. Under the leadership of the Commonwealth Secretariat and Foundation, myriad agencies and organs of the Commonwealth carry out different types of aid giving to a wide range of Commonwealth partners, on the basis of region, poverty-eradication goals and thematic goals. Like the EU, the Commonwealth views aid as crucial to its soft power. It too has a normative template comprising the values of democracy, the rule of law, human rights and good governance; and while it cannot deploy the same modes of conditionality, Commonwealth giving has been credibly historic and equitable—even though the quantity of giving is unsurprisingly much more limited than major funders such as the EU or USAid—flowing out of a small budget of £49 million, funded largely by the UK, Canada and Australia.[8]

There, however, the comparisons must end. The Commonwealth is arguably an aid giver of impressive and long-standing repute. Yet the inputs and soft power outputs of its aid have failed to impress in a number of quarters. The inputs suffer from two key failings: first, a lack of clarity with the norms to be imparted, i.e. the way in which specific tranches of aid are designed to act as vehicles of normative reform; and second, the tangibility of outcomes, for both the recipient state and the Commonwealth as a whole. As stated by Gruenbaum, a recent Wilton Park report made the following vital points:

> The Commonwealth can also promote positive economic outcomes and prosperity through better enforcing its values. Values enshrined in the Commonwealth Charter … all have important implications for prosperity in Commonwealth member states … The Commonwealth must not lose sight of its values and morals, which should underpin its approach to economic growth. (Gruenbaum, 2014, p. 370)

Second, there currently exists an unclear understanding regarding the use of advocacy work by various Commonwealth actors to make a genuine impact via their 'highly developed and well-established networks of "the people's Commonwealth"' to affect civil societies, in public and private sectors (Government Response to the House of Commons, 2013, p. 12). Thus, despite the universality (and presumably suitability) of civilisational and transformative norms being propounded to Commonwealth members, and the formidable non-diplomatic contacts afforded through Commonwealth groups targeting civil society, there is now a profound *norm–aid disconnect*, which subsequently causes an undoing of the soft power of the Commonwealth as an institution.

A helpful exercise by which to gain a proper sense of this norm–aid disconnect, and the subsequent undermining of the overall soft power impetus of the Commonwealth, is to examine any major report of the Commonwealth's aid structures, over a two- or three-year period. The UK's Department for International Development (DFID) produces many such reports, the most notable being the *Multilateral Aid Review*, which in 2011 and 2013 concluded that Commonwealth aid giving was not strictly fit for purpose, and that its overall diplomatic efficacy, as far as soft power impact was concerned, was subsequently attenuated. Using criteria including both the Commonwealth Secretariat's contribution to UK development objectives[9] and organisational strengths[10] to measure a range of sub-criteria, including *criticality to international objectives*, *partnership behaviour* and *cost and value consciousness*, the Secretariat's ability to 'help … to uphold democratic values across the Commonwealth' and small-state representation was deemed in the 2011 report to be neither 'critical in delivering UK developing objectives' (DFID, 2011, p. 83) nor satisfactory in terms of strategic focus, transparency and results-based management. The latter is a particularly tough task for even the most skilled of aid actors, to be sure, but it is rendered virtually impossible in the absence of commitment to its normative template of a decent strategic focus on delivering key programmes. The Commonwealth Secretariat's Development Programmes, despite their 'unique role in the international system in supporting the wide range of development networks ...[and] significant potential, especially given the breadth of its partnerships, and its commitment to democratic values' thus achieved in 2011 an 'unsatisfactory' rating (p. 169). The Commonwealth Secretariat's Development Programmes failed to contribute to the UK's development objectives primarily because of the variability of its own mechanisms, its lack of formal policies with fragile states and its lack of focus on results—failing further because of inadequate organisational strengths including short-lived projects with no follow-up, weak country-level partnerships, and 'little evidence of a series commitment cost control' (ibid.). With neither formal fragile state policies nor country-specific development action plans, it is little wonder that the Commonwealth Secretariat struggles to make development aid effective in the majority of its recipient states.

The European Development Fund, by contrast, received strong 2011 results in both its contribution to UK development objectives (something of interest for the UK's anti-EU constituency) and its own organisational strengths (DFID, 2011, p. 9). The former signifies the ongoing soft power ability of the EU, precisely because it has systematically addressed extant norm–aid disconnects; the latter represents an obvious source of good practice for Commonwealth Secretariat staff in terms of a complete overhaul of development policy motives, modes and methods, as well as easing the challenge of the 'major reform' demanded of the Commonwealth Secretariat in the 2011 DFID report, and echoed again in the 2013 report. The year 2013 saw a small but important change, with the Commonwealth Secretariat moving from the lowest score possible—representing 'poor value for money'—to the second lowest score, noting gradual improvements in financial management, but still lacking any strategic ability to produce a credible performance as an aid giver, with 'little or no progress in its contribution to development objectives' (DFID, 2013, p. 119).

As subsequently argued in the 2013 Government Response to the House of Commons on the role and future of the Commonwealth, 'while the Commonwealth could potentially play a significant role in development, the Secretariat lacked focus in its activities and its potential was not being realised' (p. 8). Beneath the heading 'losing credibility on development', the report noted with some alarm that

> [t]he Commonwealth's performance as a provider of development aid has been disappointing in recent years, and needs to improve substantially if its reputation is to be restored. We look to the UK Government to keep the development performance of the Secretariat under close scrutiny and to keep to its stated intention to provide further funding only on convincing evidence of improvement. (Government Response to the House of Commons, 2013, p. 14)

The government's attitude here has been informed not only by above-mentioned DFID reports, but also by a slew of rising discontent among other members and observers. The most recent example of this was the decision in spring 2013 of the Canadian government to suspend its annual voluntary contribution to the Secretariat's Commonwealth Fund for Technical Cooperation (CFTC) (amounting to $10 million CDN), a decision taken—in the words of Canadian High Commissioner Gordon Campbell—to indicate Canada's displeasure with the Commonwealth, which, in 'turning away from its principles … has reached a low point in its history and is simply not fulfilling its values-based vocation' (Campbell, 2014, p. 1).

The point is crucial: failing to operate as a decent aid provider undermines the specific normative template that the Commonwealth represents to its members and to the world as a whole; this in turn drastically undermines the ability of the Commonwealth to operate as a soft power actor within the international community. To preserve its own soft power, both sides of the norm–aid disconnect need to be remedied swiftly by the Commonwealth; the former in order to *preserve* its own normative integrity, the latter in order to *reserve* the ability to have a beneficial impact through generosity.

Thus, despite the enthusiastic advocacy of its supporters, including Lord Howell of Guildford, who spoke both eloquently and passionately in the June 2011 issue of *The Round Table* of the Commonwealth as an 'unparalleled international organisation' and the 'world's best soft power network' (Howell, 2011, p. 251), it is increasingly clear that the Commonwealth has dropped the ball. Quite apart from its normative integrity as a proponent of civilisational values, which even the EU will admit is a tough task at the best of times, on the more instrumental task of simply allotting funds and keeping systematic contact with members in official diplomatic and unofficial advocacy-group terms, the Commonwealth has proved unfocused, disorganised, and worse—disinclined to make amends. This is a pity, because there is precious little else to constitute Commonwealth soft power.

While a Commonwealth investment group may gain traction (particularly if good governance can spur on decent foreign direct investment in key members), even the most rudimentary understanding of World Trade Organisation provisions makes clear that ideas of a Commonwealth trading network are inopportune at best and wholly impractical at worst. The best that could be hoped for in this case is for Commonwealth members to press the case with the UK government to remain firmly within the EU, for the benefit of any free trade agreements that could be negotiated on their behalf by the EU, brokered by the UK as a middleman. The Commonwealth Secretariat in particular needs to identify niche areas where it can be of genuine assistance, for example: encouraging a healthy investment climate in private sectors and a credible normative climate in the public sector of its members; and sanctioning breaches, but also assisting in capacity building, e.g. on the basis of similar legal and/or parliamentary systems. Stable national institutions and robust, non-corrupt business environments, underwritten by rule of law for the former and strong public procurement mechanisms in the latter, are a good start.

In terms of overhauling aid, a number of action points need to be followed. Secretariat reform first and foremost, followed by a serious overhaul of aid giving to target the most poverty-stricken member states in a way that prevents the state itself from absorbing Commonwealth funds illicitly. Brokerage to ensure that the right part of 'recipient chain' is targeted, by working in tandem with extant and experienced aid givers, could be a good start. Budget cutting through a serious embarkation on co-location of embassies and consular representations constitutes another helpful measure.[11] Shaw's comparative approach is particularly instructive here. He notes that Commonwealth entities 'are more than formal institutions: they advance a wide range of compatible networks which would not exist as they do today without the foundational support of the Commonwealths' (Shaw, 2010, p. 334). As such, seeking to 'exploit their respective Commonwealth connections in terms of their foreign policies and economic connections' would produce pursuable, manageable collaborations, particularly in the area of development aid between former French and British dependencies, all of whom now 'seek to relate to the EU as it progresses beyond the asymmetrical African, Caribbean and Pacific (ACP) era to one of formally symmetrical Economic Partnership Agreements (EPAs)' (Shaw, 2010, p. 336).

Exporting 'House Values': Moral Suasion or Normative Persuasion?

The European Union

When it comes to norms, Europe remains a key 'embodiment of soft power' (Cooper, 2003, p. 167), with an ability to project norm-based, aid-funded and diplomatically linked soft power in its immediate neighbourhood and beyond. The EU has, since its formal inception as a political entity under the Maastricht Treaty of 1993, operated on the basis of a clear set of basic principles (democracy, rule of law, human rights), thematic strategies (e.g. sustainable development) and procedural norms (e.g. good governance) (Melissen, 2005, p. 126). To its members, the EU struggles daily to keep these norms salient in the face of economic turbulence and foreign policy fallout that seems closer and closer to home, at times. Preaching the 'incalculable' benefits of membership in terms of liberal markets, freedom-based opportunities and harmonised policies, all of which at some point appear apposite to national policies, has proven to be the toughest challenge yet for EU and national leaders alike (Marshall, 1998, p. 362).

Its greatest achievement is likely to be the continued promoting of clearly defined norms and the ongoing challenge of defending them in the form of various foreign policies, whether self-standing aid-based projects, or increasingly 3-D holistic programmes that overlap principles and practices. Spectacular failures, in the form of the European Neighbourhood Policy (targeting the 16 states that surround the EU to the south and east), have caused serious soul-searching, while quiet successes in the Balkans, Israel–Palestine, Iranian nuclear proliferation, and discernible aid-based change have produced a commitment to continue exporting the EU's normative template. The EU holds a relatively healthy, but frequently impaired scorecard, therefore, in terms of its effectiveness as a soft power.

The Commonwealth

The Commonwealth has a tougher time. Its Charter is younger, less judicially potent than the EU's body of treaties and secondary legislation, its strategies far less developed in terms of country-to-country engagement. Critics suggest it labours under the shadow of the past; supporters argue that it has transcended it. Either way, the case for membership remains clouded by heritage; as such, its value-based (normative) template is less sure-footed than that espoused by the UN, the EU, or even funding or security institutions such as the European Bank for Reconstruction and Development (ERBD), the Organisation for Economic Cooperation and Development or NATO. The Commonwealth has worked well, albeit tardily, to institutionalise the implicit: to make clear that the Commonwealth Secretariat represents the values long held by the Commonwealth Foundation and myriad other Commonwealth actors. Although there is an undoubted value-based structure operating as the founding structure of the Commonwealth, the problem is twofold. The substantive issue is that few Commonwealth members seem to interpret and govern according to the same values as those defined in the Commonwealth Charter. Breaches of human rights, infractions of the rule of law, and uneven democratic practices characterise fully two-thirds of Commonwealth membership, and have for years, from anti-gay legislation to corruption, from anti-gender balance to manifestly unlawful treatment of swathes of civil society.

There is therefore an abiding and corrosive *normative disconnect* at the heart of the Commonwealth, which is frequently deemed too politically sensitive to talk about. This far outflanks the procedural difficulties of a *norm–aid disconnect* in which the Commonwealth struggles to identify the value-base upon which, or at least alongside which, it operates as an aid actor and civil society advocate. As argued above, the EU learned this lesson the hard way: having conspicuously failed to strike proactive allegiances with its Mediterranean and central European neighbours in the past five years, it now confronts a dangerously unstable neighbourhood whose key members remain in varying degrees of revolt. The normative centre of the EU—at least as regards its affiliated neighbour 'partners'—is at times perilously close to coming unstuck: all for want of identifying normative dissonances and failing to build practical, cross-cultural bridges.

Equally, Commonwealth decision-makers need to display more in the way of a pragmatic understanding of the challenges facing developing states. This does not equate with infinite patience in the face of infractions, but rather, as articulated recently by Deputy Secretary-General of the Commonwealth Secretariat Mmasekgoa Masire-Mwamba, an appreciation of the ongoing need within African member states for the Commonwealth to 'use soft power and its status as a trusted power' (Chatham House, 2014, p. 3). Masire-Mwamba suggested that the Commonwealth's hybrid mix of official and non-official structures was a key strength, allowing it to 'entrench a culture of democracy and embrace Commonwealth values' in a top-down manner (e.g. via the benchmarks of the Latimer House Principles), while supporting the economic, democratic requirements of national societies in bottom-up strategies including election observers and parliamentary expertise (as found in the Commonwealth Election Network). Taken together, the Commonwealth could expertly leverage soft power to build 'the link between development and democracy', holding national leaderships accountable while ensuring reliable support for multi-sector capacity building (Chatham House, 2014, p. 3).

The second problem is procedural. Simply put, because of its voluntary and non-binding membership basis, the Commonwealth remains ineffectual in being able to sanction identifiable breaches against its normative Charter. The only repercussion is full suspension, a reaction so robust that it is rarely used. Without a ready spectrum of available political, diplomatic and economic responses targeting both official and unofficial sources, the Commonwealth—despite the high irony of being deeply plugged into the make-up of its member states—has few foreign policy tools with which to signal a range of approval or dissatisfaction. This suggests that the Commonwealth projects only positive soft power: rewarding good behaviour with hub-spoke support but failing to sanction infractions, whether periodic or chronic. This in turn weakens the normative foundation underwriting the Commonwealth entity. The options are few: the vaunted 'quiet diplomacy' used persuades members of the virtues of non-binding observance (which runs the risk of being ineffectual at best and transparent at worst); or an institutionalised disregard of clear breaches because of an absence of targeted diplomatic tools

THE COMMONWEALTH AND THE EUROPEAN UNION IN THE 21ST CENTURY

(which erodes the normative integrity of the Commonwealth as an entity and steadily weakens its ability to project any soft power combination upon its members).

Ironically, the impartiality of the Commonwealth, coupled with its 'resilience and adaptability' (Howell, 2011, p. 252), may be part of the problem. The EU has suffered from failing to halt giving in the face of periodic breaches. The Commonwealth, however, has failed to halt giving, assistance and membership in the face of breaches both flagrant and persistent. This is both a breach in terms of the norms of the Commonwealth (housed, *inter alia*, in the Commonwealth Charter) that are not upheld, and a contravention of the basic rules and regulations by which the Commonwealth accords aid. We cannot judge the Commonwealth harshly for failing to withhold aid from states who breach cardinal values, largely because it does not operate the same mechanisms of conditionality as does the EU; but we can, and indeed should, judge the Commonwealth for failing to withdraw any of its varied aid support, on the basis of its own rules, in the face of such breaches. The upshot is that despite both its diplomatic and non-diplomatic networks, the 'excellent opportunities for the exercise of "soft power"' are being squandered (Government Response to the House of Commons, 2013, p. 12).

Conclusions

This article arrives at a variety of interesting, if rather unwieldy conclusions. The Commonwealth clearly remains an engaged, cosmopolitan institution of states with a surprisingly robust range of official and non-official contacts that leverage a series of aid and advocacy approaches across its members. However, its normative value-base, alongside these aid and advocacy tools, has not yet transformed the Commonwealth into an effective soft power. This is explained by lukewarm strategy flowing from the Commonwealth Secretariat and the apparent diffidence of Commonwealth members to the overall value of the organisation.

The EU emerges better in comparison; no longer a 'club of superficially like-minded countries' but a burgeoning union of states, a regional and sometime international actor, with a veritable plethora of foreign policies. Equally however, as manifested by events still unfolding in the European Neighbourhood Area to its south and east, the soft power of the EU has clear limits. Economic incentives, civil society support and general normative appeal are not yet a potential enough soft power cocktail to guarantee policy success in all quarters at all times.

As outlined above, a great deal of institutional sharing could take place, particularly in the area of shared development goals. As I suggested in May 2014 in my keynote speech to the Royal Commonwealth Society of Canada, the Commonwealth should take seriously the prospect of connecting more formally with the EU, and working proactively with DG DevCo and the European External Action Service, as well as with various configurations of the Council of the European Union (e.g. General Affairs Council, the Foreign Affairs Council, EcoFin, etc.). The challenge is to transform the Commonwealth from a tacit network into an active soft power; from a normative base that remains largely implicit, to an explicit purveyor of official and unofficial support to a range of developed and developing states. Neither the Commonwealth, nor its advocates, nor its critics (Clark 2013), should be content with the suggestion that its 'relative insignificance' provides it with flexibility: it does not (Shaw, 2010, p. 344).

THE COMMONWEALTH AND THE EUROPEAN UNION IN THE 21ST CENTURY

Insignificance is the step before obsolescence. Nor should the Commonwealth permit the continuance of behaviour from members that represent 'pragmatic political cultures' (Shaw, 2010, p. 344). Members work to uphold what they signed up to officially; if not, then the unofficial Commonwealth may find itself the unhappy inheritor of serious bridge-building tasks in an association characterised by *norm–norm disconnect*. Scholars in turn bear the responsibility of producing decent research on the policy options open to the Commonwealth, and its ability to key in its distinctive set of networks to 21st century global governance (Shaw and Ashworth, 2010).

The final word goes to the in-depth scrutiny flowing from the House of Lords Select Committee on Soft Power and the UK's Influence, whose 2013–14 report makes clear that soft power is an indispensable part of the make-up of contemporary state actorness. Understanding soft power simply as 'generating international power through influencing other countries to want the same things as the UK', the main method is the construction of international relations and coalitions 'which defend our interests and security, uphold our national reputation and promote our trade and prosperity' (House of Lords, 2014, p. 5).

Both the EU and the Commonwealth emerge not only as key relationships in this respect, but also representative of the soft power platforms that can be used effectively to defend both Britain's and their own value sets. Alongside other 'networks of the future', the Lords suggested that, despite the urgent need for reform, there was 'new significance for the UK of the modern Commonwealth, offering high-growth and high-savings markets, as well as a gateway to many of the great emerging powers of Asia, Africa and Latin America … not quite understood in Whitehall … [and that] education, business, training and cultural sectors have taken the lead in Commonwealth networking' (House of Lords, 2014, p. 12). The opportunities are immeasurable and the stakes have never been higher. What is needed is an 'updating' of the 'strong narrative' informing the world of the Commonwealth's vibrancy and viability, rather than endless discourses about potential. What holds for the UK will arguably hold for the Commonwealth, namely that with such narrative focusing, the soft power of the Commonwealth 'will only achieve real momentum' if it achieves and maintains a renewed 'sense of purpose' (House of Lords, 2014, p. 18). The Commonwealth can then, and only then, become the 'ideal global platform for the 21st century' as so passionately elucidated by Lord Howell (2011, p. 252).

Acknowledgement

Commune Consensu, 'By common consent'. With many thanks to Michel Gloznek, MPhil, St Antony's College, Oxford, former Canterbury Christ Church Politics/IR student, and a recent convert to all things Commonwealth.

Notes

1. Shaw identifies four commonwealth entities: Anglophone, Francophone, Lusophone and Iberoamerican states.
2. Nye (2004, 2011), Melissen (2005), Leonard (2005), and many others.
3. Nye argues that soft power 'rests primarily on three resources': culture, political values and foreign policies (Nye, 2004, p. 11). In addition, entities like the EU, which represent an economic and monetary

THE COMMONWEALTH AND THE EUROPEAN UNION IN THE 21ST CENTURY

union equivalent to its political pulling power, are further characterised by 'sticky power', which denotes the specific influence of economy in terms of trade, currency and investment (Melissen, 2005, p. 33).

4. Normative power has produced equal amount of scholarship as has soft power. However, where soft power remains a generic concept applicable to a range of international actors, the derivation and application of normative power is almost exclusively European in genealogy, with Carr, Duchêne, Galtung, Manners and Whitman–and many more–contributing to this debate.

5. Macrocosms of this same generic–genetic problem are found in the multilateral versus bilateral approach to foreign policies, while microcosm examples are represented in the regional versus state-specific approach attempted in key policies such as trade, security and even diplomacy by various international organisations.

6. European Union development policy is a complex, fast-moving and intricate area of scholarship. Key readings in this field include, for example, Carbone (2009), Gerrit and Orbie (2009), Flint (2008), Holden (2009) and Mold (2007).

7. At various stages of negotiation and completion, the five African EPAs comprise West Africa, Central Africa, Eastern and Southern Africa, the Eastern African Community and the South African Development Community; with one Caribbean and one Pacific EPA grouping (European Union, 2015).

8. The Foreign and Commonwealth Office pays the UK's share of the Secretariat's regular budget, while DFID funds the two main development programmes: the CFTC and the Commonwealth Youth Programme.

9. Encompassing seven sub-criteria of criticality to international objectives, criticality to UK aid objectives, focus on poor countries, fragile contexts, gender equality, climate change/environment, and contribution to net results.

10. Encompassing five sub-criteria of cost and value consciousness, partnership behaviour, strategic performance, financial resources management, and transparency and accountability.

11. As suggested in the 2013 Government Response to the House of Commons (p. 11), 'co-location of Embassies, where it is of mutual benefit, supports closer cooperation, as well as leading to efficiency savings'.

References

Campbell, G. (2014) Commonwealth in crisis: Canada's call for the Commonwealth to respect its core values and principles, *The Round Table*, 103(5), pp. 517–519.

Carbone, M. (Ed.) (2009) *Policy Coherence and EU Development Policy*. London and New York: Routledge.

Chatham House, The Royal Institute of International Affairs (2014) Africa programme summary, *Commonwealth Diplomacy in Africa: A Case for Trusted Partnersips and Soft Power*. London.

Cini, M. and Perez-Solorzano Borragan, N. (Eds.) (2009) *European Union Politics*. Oxford: Oxford University Press.

Clark, C. (2013) Harper raises stakes by threatening to cut Commonwealth funding, *The Globe and Mail*, 7 October, http://www.theglobeandmail.com/news/politics/harper-scrubs-sri-lanka-visit-over-human-rights-violations/article14719839/, accessed 15 March 2015.

Cooper, R. (2003) *The Breaking of Nations: Order and Chaos in the Twenty-first Century*. New York: Atlantic Books.

Department for International Development (2011) *Multilateral Aid Review: Ensuring Maximum Value for Money for UK Aid through Multilateral Organisations*. London (March).

Department for International Development (2013) *Multilateral Aid Review: Driving Reform to Achieve Multilateral Effectiveness*. London (December).

European Union (2012) EPAs: still pushing the wrong deal for Africa?, http://www.stopepa.de/img/EPAs_Briefing.pdf, accessed 15 March 2015.

European Union (2013) Preliminary data on 2013 official development assistance, http://europa.eu/rapid/press-release_MEMO-14-263_en.htm, accessed 15 March 2015.

European Union (2014) The European Union explained: international co-operation and development, http://europa.eu/pol/pdf/flipbook/en/development_cooperation_en.pdf, accessed 15 March 2015.

European Union (2015) Overview of EPA negotiations, http://trade.ec.europa.eu/doclib/docs/2009/september/tradoc_144912.pdf, accessed 15 March 2015.

Ferguson, N. (2003) Power, *Foreign Policy*, 134(1), pp. 18–22, p. 24.

THE COMMONWEALTH AND THE EUROPEAN UNION IN THE 21ST CENTURY

Flint, A. (2008) *Trade, Poverty and the Environment: The EU, Cotonou and the African–Caribbean–Pacific Bloc*. Hampshire: Palgrave Macmillan.

Gerrit, F. and Orbie, J. (Eds.) (2009) *Beyond Market Access for Economic Development: EU–Africa Relations in Transition*. London and New York: Routledge.

Government Response to the House of Commons (2013) Foreign Affairs Committee Report HC1114 of Session 2012–13, *The Role and Future of the Commonwealth*. London: Cm 8521 (January).

Gruenbaum, O. (2014) Commonwealth update, *The Round Table*, 103(4), pp. 369–374.

Hadfield, A. (2007) Janus advances? An analysis of EC development policy and the 2005 amended Cotonou partnership, *European Foreign Affairs Review*, 12(1), pp. 39–66.

Holden, P. (2009) *In Search of Structural Power: EU Aid Policy as a Global Political Instrument*. Farnham and Burlington: Ashgate.

Hoover Institution Stratford University (2012) Power and weakness, by Robert Kagan, http://www.hoover.org/publications/policy-review/article/7107, accessed 9 November 2012.

House of Lords (2014) *Select Committee on Soft Power and the UK's Influence, Report of Session 2013–2014, Persuasion and Power in the Modern World*. London: The Stationery Office.

Howell, Lord and of Guildford (2011) The Commonwealth: a global network of the 21st century, *The Round Table*, 100(414), pp. 251–255.

Hurt, S. (2010) Understanding EU development policy: history, global context and self-interest?, *Third World Quarterly*, 31(1), pp. 159–168.

Khanna, P. (2012) The persistent myths of 'soft power', *LSE Political Science Blog*, http://blogs.lse.ac.uk/ideas/2012/01/the-persistent-myths-of-soft-power/, accessed 15 September 2014.

Leonard, M. (2005) *Why Europe will Run the 21st Century?* London: Fourth Estate.

Manners, I. (2002) Normative power Europe: a contradiction in terms?, *Journal of Common Market Studies*, 40(2), pp. 235–258.

Marshall, P. (1998) The United Kingdom, the Commonwealth, the European Union, *The Round Table*, 87 (347), pp. 357–365.

Melissen, J. (Ed.) (2005) *The New Public Diplomacy: Soft Power in International Relations*. Hampshire: Palgrave Macmillan.

Meyer, C.O. (2006) *The Quest for a European Strategic Culture*. Basingstoke: Palgrave Macmillan.

Mold, A. (Ed.) (2007) *EU Development Policy in a Changing World: Challenges for the 21st Century*. Amsterdam: Amsterdam University Press.

Moravcsik, A. (2010) Europe, the second superpower, *Current History*, 109(725), pp. 91–98.

Niemann, A. and Bretherton, C. (2013) EU external policy at the crossroads: the challenge of actorness and effectiveness, *International Relations*, 27(3), pp. 261–275.

Nye, J.S. (2004) *Soft Power: The Means to Success in World Politics*. New York: Public Affairs.

Nye, J.S. (2011) *The Future of Power* New York: Public Affairs.

Shaw, T. (2010) Comparative Commonwealths: an overlooked feature of global governance?, *Third World Quarterly*, 31(2), pp. 333–346.

Shaw, T. and Ashworth, L.M. (2010) Commonwealth perspectives on international relations, *International Affairs*, 86(5), pp. 1149–1165.

Van Reisen, M. (2007) The enlarged European Union and the developing world, in A. Mold (Ed.), *EU Development Policy in a Changing World: Challenges for the 21st Century*. Amsterdam: Amsterdam University Press.

Wilson, E.J. (2008) Hard power, soft power, smart power, *Annals of the American Academy of Political and Social Science*, 616, pp. 110–124.

The Commonwealth of Nations and the EU after the 'Global' Crisis: Rethinking Post-2015 'Global' Development?

TIMOTHY M. SHAW

Visiting Professor, Aalborg University, and University of Massachusetts Boston, Boston, USA

ABSTRACT   *The continuing 'global' crisis has accelerated divergences between regions, especially between the 'rising' global South, the European Union (EU) of the PIIGS (Portugal, Ireland, Italy, Greece and Spain) and Cyprus, which belongs to both the Commonwealth and the EU. This article studies the emerging 'vertical' divergences between the EU and the global South, especially around the so-called Economic Partnership Agreements, and the parallel 'horizontal' divergences among Anglophone, Francophone (the Organisation Internationale de la Francophonie) and Lusophone (the Comunidade dos Países de Língua Portuguesa) Commonwealths, with their inheritance of emulation and competition. It focuses on the possibilities of enhanced human/citizen security to propose an analysis that challenges established perspectives and points towards prospects for Commonwealth 'schools' of international relations/development.*

Introduction

> Past literature on the Commonwealth has been overwhelmingly descriptive, historical and lacking in theoretical substance. It has also, perhaps like the Commonwealth itself, sought to avoid controversy and has been largely devoid of any strong critical reflection on the organization. (Taylor, 2000, p. 51)

> The [Sen] Commission believes that the response to confrontational problems should be rooted in the Commonwealth's agreed fundamental emphasis on human rights, liberties, democratic societies, gender equality, the rule of law and a political culture that promotes transparency, accountability and economic development. It is important to appreciate that the Commonwealth is not just a family of nations; it is also a family of peoples. Furthermore, the Commonwealth provides a forum in which governments and civil society meet as partners and as equals. With over 85 pan-Commonwealth professional associations and civil society organizations,

THE COMMONWEALTH AND THE EUROPEAN UNION IN THE 21ST CENTURY

the Commonwealth family connects through institutional as well as personal links, and operates through cultural as well as political, social and economic affiliations.

Drawing on the participation and consultation with its civil society partners, the Commonwealth makes decisions on the basis of negotiation, dialogue, precedent and consensus. This so-called 'Commonwealth approach' of working ensures that members respect each other and try to understand, as fully as possible, the points of view of others. (Commonwealth Secretariat, 2007, pp. 9–10)

The transnational perspective has attracted considerable support within the emerging field of global studies. (O'Bryne and Hensby, 2011, p. 175)

This article seeks to analyse several essentially 'transnational' perspectives (Hale and Held, 2011) on the Commonwealths (pluralised to reflect their very heterogeneous character), inter- and non-state, formal and informal, official and otherwise. It therefore intends to go beyond multilateralisms to cultural, education, development, global governance networks, regional security, technology, transnational studies and genres. As I recently suggested: 'The Commonwealth brings together four or five regions, comprises non-state as well as state actors, and reaches out to non-formal connections (such as Commonwealth literature or film, sports—not just Commonwealth Games but also cricket and rugby—and myriad diasporas, especially in the North)' (Shaw, 2011, p. 311).

The balance between inter- and non-governmental relations in the Commonwealths means that they are quite amenable to 'transnational' perspectives (Khagram and Levitt, 2007), which treat all diverse cross-border relations, including the informal and the illegal. In turn, they have been innovative in advancing forms of 'transnational governance' (Hale and Held, 2011) in which a set of heterogeneous actors—non-state as well as state—identify, mobilise around and attempt to manage proliferating 'global issues' such as climate change, conflict diamonds and small arms, to cite but a few examples, as well as various forms of fundamentalism, extremism and terrorism. As the Commonwealths have a tradition of bridging the inter- and non-state gap, and as the 'empires' had economic dimensions as well as social and strategic ambitions, they have been able to advance features such as corporate social responsibility with relative ease through, for instance, the Commonwealth Business Council. Perhaps the most telling of such Commonwealth achievements is the Kimberley Process to control 'blood diamonds': corporations and governments, cities and industrial groups, labour groups and consumers in Australia, Botswana, Canada, India, Namibia, South Africa as well as Britain were central to the creation and implementation of the Kimberley Process—particularly in the shaping of evaluation and sanctions and in giving it publicity (Hale and Held, 2011). In turn, such resonance with transnational approaches can advance the notion of 'global studies', which transcends established disciplines and debates, as indicated in the citation from O'Bryne and Hensby (2011) above.

The inter-state membership of the Commonwealth of Nations is concentrated in a half-dozen regions—including Europe (with Cyprus, Malta and the United Kingdom)—and the Overseas Territories (OTs) are concentrated in the Caribbean and the Pacific. Commonwealth states constitute the majority of the member states of the Caribbean Community (CARICOM), the East African Community (EAC), the Indian Ocean Rim

THE COMMONWEALTH AND THE EUROPEAN UNION IN THE 21ST CENTURY

Association (IORA), the Organisation of Eastern Caribbean States (OECS), the Pacific Island Forum (PIF), the Southern African Development Community (SADC), the South Asian Association of Regional Cooperation (SAARC) and the Southern African Custom Union (SACU). They are also a central force in the African, Caribbean and Pacific group of states (ACP) (Shaw, 2011). In turn, their distinctive relations might be said to constitute a 'Commonwealth school' of international and/or transnational relations (Shaw and Ashworth, 2010). Such an approach privileges non-state rather than inter-state relations, many of which are concentrated at the regional or sub-global level, such as informal trade, human mobility, mobile-phone connectivity, sports competitions or water governance.

Even though the European Union (EU) recognises 34 Overseas Countries and Territories of six of its (post-colonial) members, groupings such as small island developing states (SIDS) and the ACP in which the Commonwealth dimension is paramount are no longer central to an EU of 28 heterogeneous members which is preoccupied by the never-ending eurozone crisis, Russia's interventions in Ukraine, the regional conflicts around Syria, the Kurds, ISIS and Turkey, and the apparent radicalisation of religious communities inside the EU compounded by anti-immigration forces.

Further, the unexpected decline in the prices of commodities and energy as well as in the value of some currencies suggests that the global dynamo of the BRICS (Brazil, Russia, India, China and South Africa) and 'emerging markets' has weakened. The post-BRICS period is also marked by the post-Millennium Development Goals era in the United Nations (UN) and other development agencies (Shaw, 2015).

The EU and the Commonwealth in the New Post-2015 World

In the middle of the second decade of the 21st century, the Commonwealth can aspire to advance both human development and human security among and around its member countries and communities. The post-2015 Sustainable Development Goals (SDGs) agreed for the UN system are centred on 'partnerships', a quintessential Commonwealth form or norm (Taylor, 2014). This prospect is reinforced by the declining salience of the BRICS (Brazil and Russia more than China or India) and other emerging markets, as well as by the proliferation of sources of finance for development such as sovereign wealth funds, exchange-traded funds or pension funds, especially in the still-burgeoning economies in East Asia and the Gulf. This is compounded by the difficulties confronting the EU given the global crisis, especially the difficulties facing the PIIGS (Portugal, Italy, Ireland, Greece and Spain) of the eurozone, none of which are Commonwealth members, although Cyprus suffered its own idiosyncratic intense contraction in 2013. Regional rebalancing/reordering is affecting not just EU–ACP relations, with the African states feeling sufficiently empowered ('African agency'? (Shaw, 2012)) now to resist signing Economic Partnership Agreements (EPAs), unlike the Caribbean group. It is also affecting the EU's relations with Asian (Gaens, 2008), African and other regions.

The EU's ambition to sign seven EPAs with the main regions of the ACP has been frustrated by the latter's proliferating set of policy options, especially offered by the BRICS and emerging markets in the MIST group (Mexico, Indonesia, South Korea and Turkey). So only parts of West Africa have followed CARIFORUM (Caribbean Forum), with most other regions, including Eastern and Southern Africa, the Pacific and the five members of the EAC, still in protracted, very occasional talks (Commonwealth Foundation, 2008).

THE COMMONWEALTH AND THE EUROPEAN UNION IN THE 21ST CENTURY

Development think tanks in Belgium such as the Agency for Cooperation and Research in Development (ACORD) and the European Centre for Development Policy Management (ECDPM) are empathetic towards the ACP's reluctance to sign (www.acordinternational. org; www.ecdpm.org; Phillips and Weaver, 2010). Tony Heron (2013, p. 5) has treated such declines in preferences as 'the political economy of trade preference erosion'; he juxtaposes a trio of perspectives—international political economy and development, small states and global governance—to explain the ACP's adjustments. So the relatively optimistic history presented by Martin Holland and Mathew Dodge (2012) on the EU and development is increasingly in need of reconsideration. Africa's impressive growth in the 21st century owes more to the expansion of the BRICS than to the lacklustre performance or promise of the EU (Shaw, 2015) and has been increasingly internally driven by growing middle classes and their demand for mobile telecommunications, including M-Pesa facilities.

Such exponential shifts in relations between the hitherto hegemonic North Atlantic and the 'rest' (Zakaria, 2008) have led Pieterse to suggest that the established South–North axis is about to be superseded: 'the rise of emerging societies is a major turn in globalization and holds significant emancipatory potential. North–South relations have been dominant for 200 years and now an East–South turn is taking shape. The 2008 economic crisis is part of a global rebalancing process' (Pieterse, 2011, p. 22). Sean Clark and Sabrina Hoque (2012) have edited some 50 contributions, which situate the debate over the 'post-American world': what balance between change and continuity; US decline and China's rise; economy and security? In parallel, Jim O'Neill (2011) recently reviewed a decade of the BRICs (Brazil, Russia, India, China).[1] He coined the acronym at the start of the new century, but before he retired from Goldman Sachs, he preferred the 'emerging markets' of MINT/MIST (Mexico, Indonesia, Nigeria or South Korea and Turkey). Such trends and analyses advance alternative perspectives such as Parag Khanna's (2009) 'second world' and the advocacy of Khagram and Levitt (2007) and Hale and Held (2011) of transnational rather than inter-state perspectives (Gray and Murphy, 2013).

EU–ACP relations are no longer central for much of the global South, especially Africa.[2] They now have choices given the rise of 'new' donors. These include state donors, such as Brazil, China, India, Korea and/or Turkey (Cooper and Flemes, 2013). But they also include a myriad of non-state donors: faith-based organisations such as the Aga Khan Foundation, Christian Aid or World Vision (see www.ACTalliance.org); new foundations such as the Bill and Melinda Gates Foundation or the Mo Ibrahim Foundation; pension funds; private capital and exchange-traded funds such as Black-Rock; and sovereign wealth funds such as the Gulf states and Singapore which have a degree of autonomy (Richey and Ponte, 2014). Asia, especially the East Asia of the triangle of China, Japan and Korea, is coming to balance the place of the North Atlantic sphere of the US and the EU in economic, if not yet strategic, relations. Even in Africa, South Africa's regional power—though dominant in Southern Africa—is not as salient as that of, say, India or China (Shaw, 2015) in the Horn of Africa and in West Africa.

In the half-century of bipolar, nuclearised Cold War between 1945 and 1990, the 50-plus members and the Commonwealth's extensive networks of 'unofficial' non-state civil society and corporate linkages could clearly claim no such transnational, let alone inter-state, role. But in a multi-polar world in which multiculturalism and multi-faith have become ever more salient, its pattern of migrations and diasporas as well as inheritance of democratic norms and traditions might yet have something to contribute.

THE COMMONWEALTH AND THE EUROPEAN UNION IN THE 21ST CENTURY

The Commonwealth fits well with such reformulations, precisely because it was never part of post-war bipolar realism and was therefore overlooked by the US-dominated orthodox conception of international relations (IR) (Shaw, 2004; Shaw, 2010a; Shaw and Mbabazi, 2011). Its role and contribution to global development—is there such a thing as a Commonwealth 'school' of IR (Shaw and Ashworth, 2010; Shaw, 2009)?—may become more widely recognised as US political and intellectual dominance is eroded (Cox and Nossal, 2009). There are two Commonwealth members of the BRICS (India and South Africa) who have already reconnected, along with Brazil, via the democratic grouping of IBSA (India, Brazil and South Africa). Moreover, a quarter of the G20 is Commonwealth: Australia, Britain and Canada, plus India and South Africa. So the Commonwealths (state and non-state) may be more visible in and compatible with a post-American and post-realist world, even if Clark and Hoque tend to fail to contemplate them.

Bipolar perspectives have been challenged by the revival of big power competition in Russia's former sphere of influence in the Crimea in 2014 and Eastern Ukraine in 2015. In parallel, the Anglophone Commonwealth lost prestige and momentum at its lacklustre Colombo Commonwealth Heads of Government Meeting (CHOGM) in November 2013 (Baert and Shaw, 2014). However, the people or electorate in Sri Lanka subsequently handed their own surprising verdict on the increasingly undemocratic regime of Mahinda Rajapaksa's family, as the opposition candidate, Maithripala Sirisena, won the January 2015 presidential election and has been seeking to reverse constitutional and other setbacks—a symbolic reversal for the Commonwealth. Following from the lingering positive aura of the Commonwealth Games in Glasgow in mid-summer 2014, the forthcoming CHOGM in Malta in November 2015, with its theme of 'The Commonwealth—adding global value', may yet allow the Commonwealth genre to re-establish its credibility.

The historic inheritance and growing trend towards non-state actors and relations in the Commonwealth (Commonwealth Plus'? (Shaw, 2008))—private companies as well as civil societies)—point towards the development of 'network' or 'public' rather than 'club' diplomacy (Heine, 2006). At the 2015 CHOGM in Malta, the familiar trio of non-state forums—business, people's and youth—will be joined by a fourth one, specifically for women (www.chogm2015.mt).

The Commonwealth's formal membership reflects the changing global order better than its non-Anglophone parallels. The Lusophone Commonwealth (the Comunidade dos Países de Língua Portuguesa) (CPLP) comprises Brazil but La Francophonie has none of the BRICS. By contrast, the Commonwealth includes two of the five BRICS, who are also at the core of IBSA and BASIC, the coalition of China, India, Brazil and South Africa, formed at the unsuccessful or inconclusive 15th Conference of the Parties of the Copenhagen Climate Conference of December 2009. It includes several newly industrialised countries (NICs) or near-NICs, such as Singapore and Malaysia, and 'developmental states' such as Botswana or Mauritius (i.e. the 'emerging markets' discussed above). Besides, its growth in recent and imminent members features the global South: from Cameroon and Mozambique in 1995 to Rwanda in 2009 (i.e. 'frontier markets') and possibly on to Palestine or South Sudan in the coming years (Te Velde-Ashworth, 2011).

There have been surprisingly few comparative studies of the trio of 'Commonwealths' (Anglophone, Francophone and Lusophone) despite their lingering importance to the British, French and Portuguese metropoles in the EU and the generation of distinctive diasporas in Australia, Brazil, Canada, France or the United Kingdom (Shaw, 2010b,

2010c). The first pair are the more similar, stretching from rules of membership/sanctions to international games and cultural connections, but the last one has been somewhat revived by the economic ebullience of Angola, Brazil and Mozambique in contrast to Lisbon, with unemployed Portuguese now escaping economic compression at home and migrating to the far reaches of the Lusophone world.

Commonwealth connections might advance aspects of EU foreign relations, although the majority of unconnected members from Germany to Estonia, Sweden to Bulgaria might be reluctant. They are quite central to the ACP but of declining salience to the EU given the BRICS and other emerging markets such as the Next-11. Moreover, given Africa's reluctance to follow the Caribbean example and sign EPAs, and given the continuing eurozone crisis (let alone reverberations from the Arab Spring), the EU is increasingly concentrating on the burgeoning second world: relatively established, less risky 'emerging markets' as well as the newer, riskier 'frontier markets'. The EU has a series of focuses, such as the old Russian-speaking 'Commonwealth of Independent States', the Mediterranean or Asia, as well as the poorer, more fragile economies. But in Africa its democratic, environmental, labour and other conditionalities/supply chain regulations are considered excessive compared with the ease of trade with, as well as finance from, China and the other rising (Gray and Murphy, 2013) or emerging powers (Cooper and Flemes, 2013). If global reordering is cumulative, then the EU as well as the US face structural decline, exacerbated by ageing populations, while the BRICS, MINT/MIST and other emerging economies, powers, donors, societies (Pieterse, 2011) and emerging multinational corporations (MNCs) (O'Neill, 2011) enjoy growing attention and recognition.

At a comparative, macro-level, the EU and the Commonwealth can be juxtaposed in terms of contrasting regionalisms, institutionally, politically, historically and prospectively. If the latter has been distracted and diluted by the recent CHOGM in Sri Lanka, the former was already preoccupied by recent and prospective members in South and Central Europe and by Turkey. There are now 28 states including Croatia, with another half-dozen waiting in the wings, including Iceland until recently. Meanwhile, despite the continuing eurozone crisis, Latvia joined the euro as its 18th member in 2013 and so did Lithuania at the start of 2015. All the trio of Baltic economies have been in the euro from New Year's Day 2015. Together, the EU and the Commonwealth advance a 'new' regionalism approach which broadens analysis beyond the formal and inter-state context towards the informal and non-state, which even include, I would suggest, the illicit and illegal, such as human movement and trafficking, shadow banking, money-laundering and shell companies, drugs, khat and guns (Fanta *et al.*, 2013). West Africa beyond ECOWAS (Economic Community of West African States) continues to be redefined by a variety of terrorist groups, somewhat linked to al-Qaeda and Boko Haram, by transnational river valleys like the Niger, by growing drug transhipments from South America to Europe, so that its countries are in danger of becoming 'narco-states' (www.wacommissionondrugs.org), and by transnational viruses such as HIV/AIDS and now Ebola.

The CHOGM in Trinidad and Tobago in late 2009 marked the Commonwealth's 60th anniversary. Aside from a declaration confirming Commonwealth values such as democracy and development, the 21st CHOGM continued the emphasis of both the Secretariat and the Foundation on human development and security, multiculturalism and multiracialism as a response to fundamentalisms, extremisms, terrorisms, etc. This is especially so for the Foundation, whose work on 'conflict and peace-building' is

THE COMMONWEALTH AND THE EUROPEAN UNION IN THE 21ST CENTURY

more advanced and engaged than the Secretariat's on 'respect and understanding', as reflected in its communiqué from its eight 'assemblies' at Hotel Cascadia in Port of Spain. Such analysis and reflection is particularly important in ex-imperial centres, including Germany (e.g. Turkish community) and the Netherlands (e.g. Indonesian and Surinamese diasporas) as well as the United Kingdom and France. One key question, therefore, is how to encourage cosmopolitanism and multiculturalism rather than religious exclusiveness and fundamentalisms. Britain and France have a bilateral entente around conventional forces to save their budgets, including military–industrial complexes, sometimes with others in the EU as in Airbus. And both have been very engaged in their ex-colonies in West Africa over conflict/transitions, especially France in Burkina Faso, the Central African Republic, Côte d'Ivoire and Mali, and now with the Ebola pandemics—so has the US in 'its' Liberia.

The EU has had to share roles in conflicts and transitions with the Organisation for Security and Cooperation in Europe of 57 members—'the world's largest regional security organisation'—which has been particularly important in the transitions around the end of the Cold War in the old Eastern Europe and now in Ukraine. It is also closely linked to NATO, which includes Canada and the US. All three groupings have fuzzy boundaries—Norway is in Schengen but not in the EU. In short, as the title of a recent collection on the EU edited by Soren Dosenrode (2015) suggests: there are growing *Limits to Regional Integration*. Regionalisms post-2015 face myriad new issues, actors and relations symbolised by Central Europe/Asia.

The Commonwealth's association with, even advancement of, forms of human development and security may constitute an aspect of a possible Commonwealth 'School' of international relations that I have been conceptualising with Luke Ashworth (Shaw and Ashworth, 2010; Commonwealth Foundation, 2009c). This 'School' is more multilateral or global than the established 'English' one and less state-centric or realist than the hegemonic 'American' approach (Tickner and Waever, 2009). It reflects the Commonwealth's non-state antecedents and inheritance (Shaw, 2008), notably its 'transnational' inclinations, and is compatible with notions of human development, rights and security, and closely linked to the concepts of network or public rather than club diplomacy (Heine, 2006).

Such a possible perspective can be seen to be founded on the century of writing and publishing in *The Round Table*; its two commemorative collections can be seen to support such a School even if they do not make such claims themselves explicitly (May, 2010; Mayall, 2010). Such a School in policy/practice as well as in theory is reflective of the Commonwealth's continuing focus on the 'global South', reinforced by Rwanda joining in 2009, the second such member with no historic ties to Britain but rather to fellow East African Commonwealth members such as Uganda and Tanzania. The current East African Community of five is four-fifths Commonwealth; only Burundi is an outlier. Like other regions in the ACP, it has been reluctant to sign an EPA with the EU as the ACP has a range of novel policy choices and is no longer so dependent on an EU in decline.

Engaging with Human Security: Lessons from the Commonwealth?

This rest of this paper focuses on human rather than national development and security: the advancement and sustainability of community, economic, environmental, food, personal and political development and security (United Nations Development Programme, 1994, pp. 22–40). The Commonwealth was influential and visible in the

THE COMMONWEALTH AND THE EUROPEAN UNION IN THE 21ST CENTURY

anti-colonial and anti-apartheid periods, especially when Sonny Ramphal and Emeka Anyaoku were successive Secretaries-General. Despite the end of bipolarity, the Commonwealth seemed directionless and overshadowed until its 'good governance' mantra was transformed by terrorist attacks—on London transportation (7/7) as well as New York City twin towers (9/11)—in the first half of the first decade of the new century and when its cultures (social and religious as well as political and economic) were accorded a new salience.

The emphasis on 'civil paths' rather than militaristic 'wars on' drugs or terrorism seems ever more timely given the increasingly problematic character of Western military interventions in Iraq and Afghanistan, and now around Syria. Interestingly, Amartya Sen was co-chair of the UN Commission on Human Security at the start of the new millennium which led to a Human Security Unit in the Office for Coordination of Humanitarian Affairs in New York (UN, 2003). He was therefore well suited to play a similar role in the more benign context of the Commonwealth in the middle of the decade. Besides, the problematic, militaristic, unilateral US-advanced 'war on drugs' is being superseded by the 'medical' marijuana movement at home and trio of Commissions on Drugs abroad: from Latin America and global to West Africa, the latter advanced by the Kofi Annan Foundation and based in Accra, Ghana. In short, the global South has new voice or agency to refine the issue as one of health and development, not security.

Four sets of factors have encouraged the Commonwealths—inter-state Secretariat and non-state Foundation—to innovate by taking the risk of putting 'respect and understanding' and 'faith and development', respectively, on their agendas for Kampala in November 2007, leading to the 'Munyonyo Statement on Respect and Understanding' (Willis, 2009). These were further advanced at the subsequent CHOGM in Port of Spain and are compatible with, indeed integral to, the possible concept of a Commonwealth School of international relations as well as development.

First, if the Empire facilitated white migration from the mother country to the dominions, the Commonwealth has advanced new South–North migrations and the emergence of significant multiracial Commonwealth diasporas in the global North, especially Australia, Britain and Canada. Early 19th century Indian migrations under the Raj were to the Caribbean, East and Central Africa, Fiji and South Africa, with slaves and other Africans transported to the 'new' world, including the Caribbean. Older diasporas have only recently begun to rediscover their roots via new technologies and institutions such as GOPIO (Global Organisation of People of Indian Origin); newer ones such as Indians in California as well as in Australia, Britain and Canada have never quite left 'home', as they are very comfortable in two or more 'worlds'.

Second, 9/11 in the United States, 7/7 in London and the January 2015 terrorist attacks in Paris have transformed the status and image of Commonwealth and other diasporas: from legacies of empire to focuses of policy concern. Thus cricket, carnival, curry and rugby have taken on whole new meanings: bases for multicultural and multifaith frameworks to contain tendencies towards fundamentalisms and isolationism. To be sure, the Commonwealth had always been concerned about diversity, symbolised by the annual inter-faith Commonwealth Day service in London and elsewhere—recently, in March 2012, on 'Connecting Cultures'. Successive contemporary CHOGM communiqués have treated issues of 'soft' power—peace and security including peace-keeping, terrorism, responsibility to protect, human rights and the International Criminal Court, small arms and landmines, drugs, human trafficking and transnational crime.

THE COMMONWEALTH AND THE EUROPEAN UNION IN THE 21ST CENTURY

Third, the British Empire constituted something of a global security arrangement in the two World Wars, for the colonies as well as the dominions. The Second World War encouraged nationalist expressions, leading initially to the break-up of the Indian Raj and then incremental decolonisation elsewhere in Asia, Africa, the Caribbean and the Pacific. But the hold-out by white minority regimes in Southern Africa postponed and complicated the independence process until majority rule in South Africa in 1994, following the independence of Namibia in 1990. During the periods of the second and third Secretaries-General, Sonny Ramphal and Emeka Anyaoku, the Commonwealth was a focus for anti-apartheid advocacy leading, after the independence of Zimbabwe, to the articulation and agreement of a set of Commonwealth criteria for membership: from the Harare Declaration of 1991 to the Latimer House Principles of 2004. Both inter-state and non-state Commonwealths have, then, always been concerned about race and religion. But such concerns only became salient with the end of the Cold War and the contemporary rise of fundamentalisms, leading to the proliferation of terrorism. The admission of post-genocide Rwanda in late 2009 along with the reassertion of Commonwealth values in the Port of Spain Communiqué confirm that the Commonwealth is different among inter-state institutions: democratic norms, including tolerance of diversity, are prerequisites. Such an inheritance was confirmed and advanced through the 2011 Eminent Persons Group (EPG) on reform, redirection and reinvigoration. The Perth CHOGM of 2011 was particularly focused on this report and the debate which followed called for numerous—over 100—interconnected changes, some increasingly familiar, others less so: effective democracy promotion and sanctions; migrations and diasporas; small states; climate change; Secretariat–Foundation relations; and networking/partnering with unofficial/unrecognised yet respectable agencies. The Commonwealth hopes to become bolder in responding to global crisis, climate change, fundamentalisms, migration and SIDS, and the means of achieving these goals, and of connecting to UN post-2015 SDGs, is through partnerships and networks (Browne and Weiss, 2014). This seemed to lead on to a more appropriate, i.e. higher, profile among a burgeoning set of inter- and non-state agencies: branding (Te Velde-Ashworth, 2011). There was certainly controversy over some of the proposals—43 were sent to the ministerial task force for further consideration and 11 were rejected. But the EPG clearly did its work and proposed some creative directions for the Commonwealth family in the new decade whether some heads of state could concur or not.

Fourth, as the opening citation suggests, Commonwealth values privilege democracy, division of powers, gender equality, human rights, multilateralism and sustainable development. In 1995, CHOGM had established the Commonwealth Ministerial Action Group (CMAG) to advance such values and consensus-building through suspensions if necessary. It has suspended a trio of regimes to date for being insufficiently democratic —Fiji, Nigeria and Pakistan—with Zimbabwe choosing to leave in 2003 before it was re-suspended following controversial elections in 2002, followed by the Gambia in 2013. One of the more controversial proposals of the recent EPG report was the advocacy of a 'Commonwealth Commissioner for Democracy, the Rule of Law and Human Rights', who would advise the Secretariat on which regimes were flouting Commonwealth norms, to be addressed by CMAG. In other words, CMAG's agenda would no longer be decided by the inter-state body alone, but by a functional one too, which generated concerns about sovereignty infringement among the global South. A task force of ministers, however, considered those matters not accepted in Perth before the 2013

THE COMMONWEALTH AND THE EUROPEAN UNION IN THE 21ST CENTURY

CHOGM in Sri Lanka and the notion of a Commonwealth Charter was agreed. Throughout all suspensions or resignations, the Commonwealth has maintained a variety of informal communication channels, including via the 'unofficial' Commonwealth, and has become well known for its subtle 'good offices' work, as recognised in the recent comparative capacity survey of regional and other agencies in the improvement of maintenance of peace and security by UNU-CRIS (2008, p. 52).

These several strands—diasporas, histories, multilateralisms, norms—constituted the backdrop to the Commission on respect and understanding chaired by Amartya Sen (UN, 2003). The Commission itself reflected the best of the Commonwealth, and was also the first with a female majority: eminent people were drawn from all regions and fields and included Adrienne Clarkson (Canada), Noeleen Heyzer (Singapore), Wangiri Mathai (Kenya), Rex Nettleford (Jamaica) and Mamphele Ramphele (South Africa) (Shaw, 2008, pp. 92–95).

The Sen Report juxtaposed several themes from alienation and violence to respect and understanding. It recognised the history and psychology of humiliation and called for a multilateral 'Commonwealth approach', building on the Commonwealth's record of 'good offices'. It emphasised the roles of civil society and the media, particularly women's participation, along with education and sport. This is, in many ways, the Commonwealth's familiar mantra:

> Civil paths to peace, the Commission argues, are important and can be effective … the need for hard security measures does not in any way reduce the abiding relevance of pursuing the civil routes.

> The Commission argues, in particular, that there is a strong need for much more dialogue and discussion on the richness of human identities and the counterproductive nature of placing people in rigidly separated identity-boxes, linked with religion or community. The importance of people's cosmopolitan identity also demands greater recognition than it tends to get, without denying the relevance of other identities that can comfortably co-exist with a global outlook.

> At the international level, civil paths will be inescapably linked with multilateral approaches across borders …

> Accepting diversity, respecting all human beings, and understanding the richness of perspectives that people have are of great relevance for all the Commonwealth countries and for our 1.8 billion people. They are also important for the rest of the world. (Commonwealth Secretariat, 2007, pp. 13–14)

The Commonwealth's capacity in terms of new security and soft power is augmented by its tradition of engagement with culture and sports, from the annual Commonwealth Writer's Prize (now the Commonwealth Short Stories Prize) to Commonwealth Games every four years, i.e. a variety of forms of transnational relations. For example, building on diasporic film as well as Commonwealth-based Bollywood and Nollywood, reflective of extensive consultations, the Foundation produced a report in late 2009 on 'The

THE COMMONWEALTH AND THE EUROPEAN UNION IN THE 21ST CENTURY

Bigger Picture: a way forward for film in the Commonwealth'. The Sen Report called for increased attention to the media, a sector in which the non-state and private sector Commonwealths have been quite active, as reflected in overlapping professional associations such as the Commonwealth Broadcasting Association, the Commonwealth Journalists Association, Press Union and Telecommunications Organisation, several of which pre-date both Secretariat and Foundation. These transnational connections are all symptomatic of the advantages of the Anglophone Commonwealths using the *lingua franca* of globalisation: English.

Finally, as a segue into the Foundation's alternative, arguably a more radical or less cautious, perspective, Owen Willis (2009, p. 12) laments that the Sen Commission eschewed religion in terms of its contribution to either conflict or cooperation: 'The Munyonyo Statement on Respect and Understanding endorsed the Report of the Commission "which provides a thoughtful and considered analysis of issues relevant to building tolerance and understanding of diversity amongst and within distinct societies, cultures and communities." Throughout the Statement, interestingly, no mention is made directly of faith or religion.' By contrast, notes Willis, 'the Commonwealth Foundation's Report, Engaging with Faith, treats religion more sympathetically and encourages understanding and cooperation between the faith communities. The former Report may tend to treat religion as part of the problem, while the latter might view religion as part of the solution' (Willis, 2009, p. 3).

While Commonwealth heads of government considered the Sen Report in Uganda at an upmarket resort on Lake Victoria at Munyonyo, civil society received the Foundation's 'Engaging with Faith' at a modest Kampala hotel where the People's Forum was located. The Foundation's Report 'presents a sympathetic approach to religious initiatives within the Commonwealth, claiming a "growing awareness in the Commonwealth that faith-based development agencies" potential can, and do, make a special contribution to relief, peace and development' (Willis, 2009, p. 11).

Interestingly, while Willis laments the Secretariat's oversight about religion, neither report treats the private sector, or the role of the (now deceased) Commonwealth Business Council, when MNCs in war zones are increasingly engaged in efforts to contain conflict, reduce risk and improve sales and profits. However, Willis is right to chastise students of international development (and international relations) for overlooking religion as inseparable from human development and security although analysis of faith-based organisations is growing as an aspect of transnational relations, and has received increasing attention from the World Bank (Belshaw *et al.*, 2001; Clarke and Jennings, 2008). As Willis states, 'Although matters of faith, religion and spirituality are central to the lives of millions of people in the global South, and many FBOs are actively involved in development, few Northern academics in the field of international development make explicit reference to religion's role in development … However, such inattention may be changing, as religion assumes a more prominent role in the world of the 21st century' (Willis, 2009, p. 4).

Concluding Remarks

Going beyond the two 2007 documents and debates treated by Willis (2009), one of the eight 'assemblies' at the 2009 Port of Spain CHOGM was on 'conflict and peace-building'. The short background paper for this gathering was less abstract and more direct than 'Respect and Understanding' and less focused on religion than 'Engaging with Faith'. Rather, it was more domestic than comparative or global and more concerned with 'new' security issues such as gang culture and the young urban male which the current global crisis may have exacerbated. 'The goal of the Conflict and Peace-building Assembly', as the Commonwealth Foundation put it, 'is to develop concrete recommendations on how government, civil society and other stakeholders can discourage cultures of violence and promote dialogue, multilateralism, respect and understanding, particularly in fragile societies in which conflicts have occurred, are taking place or are at risk of breaking out, along identity lines' (Commonwealth Foundation, 2009a, p. 1).

Sessions planned for the two days, aside from gang culture and the urban male, included 'Current and future crises and the economics of extremism: new patterns of conflict and alienation and the financing of terror' and 'Disarmament, demobilisation and reintegration in Commonwealth post-conflict contexts'. The first pair included themes drawn from the Sen Commission such as gender and the media whereas the third, on crises, referenced new patterns of migrations and remittances, and future disputes over food, land and water. The final session on Disarmament, Demobilisation & Reintegration (of armed forces) (DDR) sought to learn from Commonwealth cases— today's Sierra Leone, Sri Lanka and Uganda, as well as Southern Africa in earlier decades—about prospects for sustainable peace, including child soldiers and small arms along with the UN's Security Council Resolution 1325 on women. In short, as the Secretariat and Foundation left Trinidad and Tobago in the last month of 2009, the Commonwealth had become more engaged than ever around issues of human security along with human development in ways not imaginable before the present century.

Memorable highlights from the Foundation's assembly included female Caribbean colleagues—Deborah Mcfee and Folade Mutota from WINAD (Women Institute for Alternative Development)—on gangs, gender and guns and a Pakistani non-governmental organisation leader on disarming young militants in Taliban training camps along the border with Afghanistan. The debate also recognised and supported UN and other multilateral measures among a variety of heterogeneous actors concerned with women, children and violence (UNSCR 1325) and on small arms and light weapons (SALW) at the turn of the decade. The Forum's non-governmental communiqué to the CHOGM (Commonwealth Foundation, 2009b) included three pages on crime and violence, armaments, education, extremism, reconciliation, refugees and networking. By contrast, the intergovernmental CHOGM treated familiar agenda items such as Belize, Cyprus, Guyana and Zimbabwe as well as CMAG issues such as Fiji along with separate sections, in order, on disarmament and arms control, SALW. terrorism, piracy, human trafficking and people smuggling, energy security and food security (Commonwealth Secretariat, 2009). These 'new' security issues have since become more salient in both Commonwealth and EU circles because of fears of fundamentalism and radicalisation.

In short, at the level of policy and practice, the CHOGM in Trinidad and Tobago at the end of the decade advanced the Commonwealth's interest in, and support of, human development and security under its then new Indian Secretary-General, Kamalesh Sharma. At the level of analysis and theory, the several related conferences in the wings of the meeting, including the centenary of *The Round Table* (May, 2010; Mayall, 2010), reinforced the embryonic conceptualisation of a Commonwealth School of IR which embraced notions of civil society, democracy, diasporas and the global South, all compatible with human development and security. In turn, they facilitated the drafting and debating of the latest EPG report at the start of the decade in Perth 2011 ('A Commonwealth of the People'?) with its transnational orientation, even if not all of its 100-plus recommendations were accepted.

But the contrast in scope and tone of the EPG on reform and partnerships stands in contrast to those around, say, the EU, the UN or international financial institutions, reflective of its modest role but also of its inheritance of a culture of collaboration: transnational governance rather than inter-state organisation. The Commonwealth, with five members in the G20, has been able more readily to absorb globalisation than its Francophone or Lusophone counterparts. It also embodies inter-regionalisms, at a time when the EU engages in its own type of intergovernmental diplomacy as an aspiring actor to advance inter-regional relations, for instance with the Association of South East Asian Nations (Shaw, 2011). The CHOGM in Malta in 2015 may thus help to bring the two diverse networks together to mutual advantage: convergence post-2015 around partnerships for SDGs?

Notes

1. Not BRICS, i.e. South Africa is not included.
2. Symptomatically, the new ACP president for 2015–20 is Dr P. I. Gomes from Guyana, and the Caribbean was the first region to agree an EPA.

References

Baert, F. and Shaw, T. M. (2014) Are you willing to be made nothing? Is Commonwealth reform possible?, *International Affairs*, 90(5), pp. 1143–1160.

Belshaw, D., Calderisi, R. and Sugden, C. (Eds) (2001) *Faith in Development: Partnership between the World Bank and Churches in Africa*. Washington, DC: World Bank.

Browne, S. and Weiss, T. W. (2014) The future UN development agenda: contrasting visions, contrasting operations, *Third World Quarterly*, 35(7), 1326–1340.

Clark, S. and Hoque, S. (Eds.) (2012) *Debating a Post-American World: What Lies Ahead?* Abingdon: Routledge.

Clarke, G. and Jennings, M. (Eds) (2008) *Development, Civil Society and Faith-based Organizations: Bridging the Sacred and the Secular*. London: Palgrave Macmillan.

Commonwealth Foundation (2008) *Breaking the Taboo: Perspectives of African Civil Society on Innovative Sources of Financing Development*. London: Commonwealth Foundation.

Commonwealth Foundation (2009a) *Commonwealth People's Forum 2009: Conflict and Peacebuilding Assembly*. London: Commonwealth Foundation.

Commonwealth Foundation (2009b) *Port of Spain Civil Society Communique to the CHOGM*. London: Commonwealth Foundation.

Commonwealth Foundation (2009c) *The Bigger Picture: A Way Forward for Film in the Commonwealth*. London: Commonwealth Foundation.

Commonwealth Secretariat (2007) *Civil Paths to Peace: Report of the Commonwealth Commission on Respect and Understanding* London: Commonwealth Secretariat.

Commonwealth Secretariat (2009) *CHOGM Communique, Port of Spain*. London: Commonwealth Secretariat.

Commonwealth Secretariat (2011) *A Commonwealth of the People: Time for Urgent Reform. A Report of the EPG to CHOGM, Perth, October 2011*. London: Commonwealth Secretariat.

Cooper, A. F. and Flemes, D. (2013) Special issue: Foreign policy strategies of emerging powers in a multipolar world, *Third World Quarterly*, 34(6), pp. 943–1,144.

Cox, W. and Nossal, K. (2009) The 'crimson world': the Anglo core, the post-imperial non-core and the hegemony of American IR, in A. B. Tickner and O. Waever (Eds), *International Relations Scholarship around the World: Worlding Beyond the West*. London: Routledge, pp. 287–307.

Dosenrode, S. (Ed.) (2015) *Limits to Regional Integration*. Farnham: Ashgate.

Gaens, B. (Ed.) (2008) *Europe–Asia Inter-regional Relations: A Decade of ASEM*. Farnham: Ashgate.

Fanta, E., Shaw, T. M. and Tang, V. (Eds) (2013) *Comparative Regional Integration for Development in the Twenty-first Century: Insights from the Global South*. Farnham: Ashgate.

Gray, K. and Murphy, C. (Eds) (2013) Special issue: Rising powers and the future of global governance, *Third World Quarterly*, 34(2), pp. 183–355.

Hale, T. and Held, D. (Eds) (2011) *Handbook of Transnational Governance*. Cambridge: Polity.

Heine, J. (2006) *On the Manner of Practising the New Diplomacy*. Waterloo: CIGI, Working Paper No. 11.

Heron, T. (2013) *Pathways from Preferential Trade: The Politics of Trade Adjustment in Africa*. London: Palgrave Macmillan.

Holland, M. and Dodge, M. (2012) *Development Policy of the EU*. London: Palgrave Macmillan.

Khagram, S. and Levitt, P. (Eds) (2007) *The Transnational Studies Reader*. New York: Routledge.

Khanna, P. (2009) *The Second World: How Emerging Powers Are Redefining Global Competition in the 21st Century*. New York: Random House.

May, A. (Ed.) (2010) *The Commonwealth and International Affairs: The Round Table Centennial Selection*. Abingdon: Routledge.

Mayall, J. (Ed.) (2010) *The Contemporary Commonwealth: An Assessment, 1996–2009*. Abingdon: Routledge.

O'Byrne, D. and Hensby, A. (2011) *Theorizing Global Studies*. London: Palgrave Macmillan.

O'Neill, J. (2011) *The Growth Map: Economic Opportunity in the BRICs and Beyond*. New York: Penguin.

Phillips, N. and Weaver, C. (Eds) (2010) *International Political Economy: Debating the Past, Present and Future*. Abingdon: Routledge.

Pieterse, J. N. (2011) Global rebalancing: crisis and the East-South turn, *Development and Change*, 42(1), pp. 22–48.

Richey, L. A. and Ponte, S. (Eds) (2014) Special issue: New actors and alliances in development, *Third World Development*, 35(1), pp. 1–195.

Shaw, T. M. (2004) The Commonwealth(s) and global governance, *Global Governance*, 10(4), pp. 499–516.

Shaw, T. M. (2008) *Commonwealth: Inter- and Non-state Contributions to Global Governance*. Abingdon: Routledge.

Shaw, T. M. (2009) Commonwealth(s) of regions extra-EU? Anglophone globalization and new regionalisms, in Ph. De Lombarde and M. Schulz (Eds), *The EU and World Regionalisms: The Makability of Regions in the 21st Century*. Farnham: Ashgate, pp. 271–285.

Shaw, T. M. (2010a) Commonwealth(s) and poverty/inequality: contributions to global governance/development, in J. Clapp and R. Wilkinson (Eds) *Global Governance, Poverty and Inequality*. Abingdon: Routledge, pp. 187–208.

Shaw, T. M. (2010b) Comparative Commonwealths: an overlooked feature of global governance, *Third World Quarterly*, 31(2), pp. 333–346.

Shaw, T. M. (2010c) Commonwealths and global development: contributions to private transnational governance?, *Commonwealth and Comparative Politics*, 48(1), pp. 91–111.

Shaw, T. M. (2011) Commonwealths and regionalisms in the first quarter of the 21st century, in T. M. Shaw, J. A. Grant and S. Cornelissen (Eds), *The Ashgate Research Companion to Regionalisms*. Farnham: Ashgate, pp. 311–323.

Shaw, T. M. (2012) Africa's quest for developmental states: renaissance for whom?, *Third World Quarterly*, 33(5), pp. 837–851.

Shaw, T. M. (2015) African agency? Africa, South Africa and the BRICS, *International Politics*, 52(2), pp. 255–268.

Shaw, T. M. and Ashworth, L. M. (2010) Commonwealth perspectives on international relations, *International Affairs*, 86(5), pp. 1149–1165.

Shaw, T. M. and Mbabazi, P. M. (2011) Civil society and accountability in the Commonwealth, in J. A. Scholte (Ed.), *Global Citizenship in Action: Civil Society and Accountable Global Governance*. Cambridge: Cambridge University Press, pp. 128–145.

Taylor, I. C. (2000) Legitimation and de-legitimation within a multilateral organization: South Africa and the Commonwealth, *Politikon*, 27(1), pp. 51–72.

Taylor, I. C. (2014) *Africa Rising? BRICS-diversifying dependency*. Woodbridge: James Currey.

Te Velde-Ashworth, V. (2011) *The Commonwealth Brand: Global Voice, Local Action*. Farnham: Ashgate.

Tickner, A. B. and Waever, O. (Eds) (2009) *International Relations Scholarship around the World: Worlding Beyond the West*. Abingdon: Routledge.

United Nations (2003) *Human Security Now: Report of the Commission on Human Security.* New York: United Nations.

United Nations Development Programme (1994) *Human Development Report 1994.* New York: Oxford University Press.

UNU-CRIS (2008) Regional and other intergovernmental organizations in the maintenance of peace and security, http://www.cris.unu.edu/fileadmin/user_upload/capacity_survey.pdf, accessed 15 March 2015.

Willis, O. (2009) Civil or religious paths to respect and understanding? Two Commonwealth reports, *The Round Table*, 98(400), pp. 3–15.

Zakaria, F. (2008) *The Post-American World.* New York: Norton.

The Commonwealth Caribbean and Europe: The End of the Affair?

PETER CLEGG
University of the West of England, Bristol, UK

ABSTRACT *The institutional relationship between the Commonwealth Caribbean and the European Union (EU) dates back to the mid-1970s, when the Lomé Convention was signed. The agreement was seen as a high water mark in First–Third World relations. However, since then the bond has come under concerted pressure. The consequence is that today the particularism that underpinned relations for so long has almost vanished and the EU is beginning to treat the Caribbean like any other relatively marginal region of the world. The article evaluates the reasons for this change, in particular: the scrapping of the trade protocols; the erosion of African, Caribbean and Pacific (ACP) preference due to free trade agreements signed by the EU; the refocusing of EU development policy towards the least developed countries; and the split in the ACP group with the creation of an ill-designed regional Economic Partnership Agreement. The article places these changes into starker relief by assessing briefly the deepening links between the United Kingdom Overseas Territories and the EU. However, as the article highlights, this link will neither reboot nor sustain the more important Commonwealth Caribbean–EU relationship.*

Introduction

The relationship between the Caribbean and Europe is undergoing real change. It is not only the independent countries of the Commonwealth Caribbean that are being affected, but also the Overseas Territories associated with the UK. However, the trajectories of the respective relationships are diverging. For some time now global pressures, new priorities and approaches in European Union (EU) development policy, and unfulfilled expectations in the Commonwealth Caribbean have all contributed to the weakening of that relationship to a point where it is now under serious threat. The article analyses the key events that have led to this situation. In particular, it considers: the ending of trade protocols; the erosion of African, Caribbean and Pacific (ACP) preference as a result of a series of free trade agreements negotiated by the EU; the refocusing of EU development policy towards the least developed countries; and the effective split in the ACP group through the establishment of a controversial regional Economic Partnership Agreement (EPA). By way of comparison the article also looks at relations between the EU and the UK Overseas Territories (UKOTs), which have actually been strengthened by

THE COMMONWEALTH AND THE EUROPEAN UNION IN THE 21ST CENTURY

the recently agreed Association of the Overseas Countries and Territories. But first the article considers the relationship between the Commonwealth Caribbean and the EU.

Where It All Began: The Lomé Conventions

When the UK joined the European Economic Community (EEC) in 1973, a key issue was what kind of relationship the Commonwealth Caribbean (from now on referred to as the Caribbean) should have with the Community. Prior to the UK's accession, the Yaoundé Convention had been agreed between the EEC and the associated states of the existing six member states, which extended Part IV of the Treaty of Rome in response to the new political and legal situation in the newly independent states. Having been signed in 1963, and renewed in 1969, the Convention was due to expire in January 1975 and so there was a good opportunity to establish a new agreement which would also incorporate the Caribbean.

The preliminary conference at which the enlarged EEC had its first discussions with the independent Caribbean countries, as well as the African Yaoundé signatories, took place in Brussels in July 1973. The Caribbean countries, in order to benefit from the expertise of their African colleagues in dealing with the EEC, initiated regular contacts and consultations with the region. This led in time to the creation of the ACP grouping, which the participants hoped would maximise the strength of their negotiating position. Indeed, the ACP felt that a fundamentally new 'association' with the EEC could be negotiated. The Caribbean wanted a form of relationship that was *sui generis* (Gonzales, 1997, p. 72). The region called for non-reciprocity, protection of traditional arrangements, and no difference in treatment between independent Caribbean countries and the self-governing territories of EEC member states in the region. In many respects, the first Lomé Convention met the objectives that the Caribbean had set itself. The aim of the Convention was 'to establish a new model for relations between developed and developing states compatible with the aspirations of the international community towards a more just and more balanced economic order' (*The Courier*, 1975, p. 3).

Lomé I was agreed in 1975, while Lomé IV was signed in 1990 and remained in force until 2000. There were three central pillars of the Lomé Conventions—trade provisions (preferences and protocols), financial aid and political dialogue. As Flint (2008, p. 14) argues, '... Lomé I appeared to offer ACP countries a number of favourable concessions. The demands for reciprocity and Free Trade Zones inherent in Yaoundé were dispensed with in favour of non-reciprocal tariff preferences for ACP countries'. Flint also calls Lomé I the 'high water mark' for ACP relations with the EU, allowing for 'a true sense of partnership' and autonomy for ACP countries over their economic policies (Flint, 2008, p. 15). Similarly, Holland and Doidge (2012, p. 55) suggest '... that the goals of the Convention were innovative and established a First–Third World relationship that was progressive and unparalleled for its time'. And despite the fact that later the EU demanded new conditions to the relationship, including on issues such as human rights, good governance and the rule of law, Lomé represented 'a singularly good deal for ACP states' (Hadfield, 2007, p. 42). Nevertheless, by the early 1990s a number of factors had combined to undermine the basis of the Lomé regime, such as doubts over its effectiveness in terms of both encouraging growth in the ACP and improving trade performance. Also, changes to the political economy of global trade, particularly the growing influence of organisations such as the newly created World Trade Organisation (WTO) '... drew

THE COMMONWEALTH AND THE EUROPEAN UNION IN THE 21ST CENTURY

attention to Lomé's inconsistencies with the broad principles of trade liberalisation', meaning '… the need for fundamental reform of the EU's relations with the ACP was becoming increasingly evident' (Holland and Doidge, 2012, p. 65).

The End of the Trade Protocols

A key development that reflected the changing approach to trade policy came in relation to the pressure on Lomé's trade protocols. The eventual scrapping of these provisions removed a central plank of the Caribbean–EU relationship. The first protocol to come under attack was the one for bananas that helped to maintain EU market access for relatively expensive Caribbean producers. Cases brought by the US and several Latin American countries at the General Agreement on Tariffs and Trade (GATT) and then at the WTO in the early and mid-1990s ripped the heart out of the protocol and the import regime. The GATT and the WTO not only ruled against certain aspects of the EU's banana regime but also questioned the legality of the preferential arrangements within the Lomé Convention. Fundamentally, they argued that the discriminatory tariffication of banana imports was against the most favoured nation (MFN) commitment, by which tariff concessions must be extended to all other members on an equal basis, and thus the Lomé Convention itself, with its preferential treatment of ACP goods, was also unlawful. The EU dismantled its banana regime and the banana protocol followed. The consequence has been a large reduction in the volume of Caribbean bananas entering the EU market and an ever-reducing tariff preference, which is the remaining legacy of the original banana regime.

With strong attacks on the banana protocol and the provisions of Lomé more generally, the other protocols were also fatally undermined. The sugar protocol went further than the one for bananas and guaranteed duty-free access to the EU market at a fixed preferential price for an agreed quota of sugar. However, in September 2002, Australia and Brazil complained to the WTO about the export subsidies provided by Brussels in its sugar regime (Thailand requested consultations with the EU on the same matter in March 2003). In October 2004, the WTO ruled that EU subsidies which benefited sugar producers in the Caribbean and elsewhere broke global trade rules. In response, the EU agreed to revise its regime in late 2005, which included a measure to phase in a 36% cut in the EU's guaranteed sugar price. Then, in September 2007, the EU announced that its sugar protocol would end entirely in 2009, which it did. In its place, Caribbean sugar exports were given duty-free access, but no guaranteed price.

More changes are planned for 2017, which will end EU production quotas and fully liberalise the market. The impact of these changes is already being felt, with recent sharp falls in the price of sugar in the EU (*The Daily Herald*, 2015). One outcome of falling prices and higher EU production may well be the end of most Caribbean sugar exports to the EU, with perhaps only Belize retaining an interest. In regard to the rum protocol, it gave bulk rum exporters from the Caribbean duty-free access under quota to the EU market. However, a deal between the EU and the US in the margins of the WTO Singapore Ministerial Meeting in March 1997 liberalised MFN duties and quotas on some categories of bottled and bulk rum entering their respective markets. As Dunlop (1999, p. 15) argued, '[t]his was negotiated without consulting ACP exporters of rum, whose competitive position has been eroded as a result'. This in turn caused Caribbean producers to experience a large reduction in exports to the EU (Cantore *et al.*, 2012).

THE COMMONWEALTH AND THE EUROPEAN UNION IN THE 21ST CENTURY

The Margin of Preference Slips Further

The preference levels for the Caribbean's key commodities have been further eroded in recent years by a growing number of free trade agreements (FTAs) signed by the EU. Woolcock (2007) argues that FTAs have been pushed because of difficulties in multilateral trade negotiations, in response to US trade policy, and due to a change of approach in the European Commission's Directorate General (DG) Trade. So the EU has signed FTAs with Colombia, Costa Rica, Mexico, South Africa and the Central American Common Market (ratification pending). Further, the EU is negotiating FTAs with MERCOSUR (Argentina, Brazil, Paraguay and Uruguay) and India.

Several studies have been undertaken to assess the impact of the FTAs on Caribbean exports. Anania (2010) looked at the implications for bananas of the FTAs between the EU and Andean and Central American countries. Anania (2010, p. 1) observed that 'the EU has agreed to progressively reduce its import tariff on bananas originating in these countries to 75 €/t'. This is below the 176 €/t at the time of the 2009 deal to end the WTO dispute, and the 114 €/t amount planned for 2019. As Aiyaz Sayed, Fiji's Minister of Industry and Trade, said, '[i]t is worth noting that these new concessions jeopardise the balance sought in the Geneva Agreement on Trade in Bananas, and completely nullifies [*sic*] some of the benefits that ACP countries could have gained from the EPAs' (ACP Press, 2012). In relation to rum, Cantore *et al.* (2012, p. vii) suggested that '... a number of planned or concluded FTAs between the EU and third countries threaten to erode [existing] preferences'. The authors contended that if the EU agreed FTAs with Central America, Peru, Colombia and MERCOSUR, Caribbean rum exports would decline at the very least by 3%, equivalent to €¾ million each year. Individual countries, such as Guyana, would be affected particularly badly. The worst case scenario would be if Central America, Peru and Colombia were allocated quotas and MERCOSUR duty-free access: losses for the Caribbean could then amount to 16.5% of exports, equivalent to about €4 million (Cantore *et al.*, 2012). Meanwhile, for sugar, the FTAs are allowing greater competition from lower cost sugar producers and this will exacerbate the Caribbean's already tenuous position in the EU market.

A final issue related to declining preference margins was the 'fateful decision' (Heron, 2014, p. 16) to implement the Everything But Arms (EBA) initiative in 2001. This covers the world's poorest countries (mostly located in Africa; with only one— Haiti—in the Caribbean) and gives duty-free access to the EU for all goods except arms and ammunition. This was an important development as it '... breached the long-established policy of offering the ACP preferential advantages over all other developing countries' (Holland and Doidge, 2012, p. 88). Concessions were made to the ACP so that duty-free access for sugar, bananas and rice would be phased in; but by 2009, free access in these sectors was established. Thus, the Caribbean ACP saw another downgrading of its preferential position.

Broader Changes in EU Development Policy

Related issues that have underpinned the changes noted above are the repositioning and refocusing of development policy within the EU. The process began in the late 1990s when plans were put in place to restructure the European Commission, which included the downgrading of the Directorate General for Development and Relations with ACP States (DG DEV). The DG, which had played a central role in supporting ACP interests, lost its responsibility for ACP trade policy. The Trade Commissioner took over that undertaking, and as a result the important link between trade and development was broken. Then, in 2010, the European External Action Service (EEAS) was established and assumed DG DEV's task for bilateral relations with the ACP countries. Within the EEAS, a Managing Directorate for sub-Saharan Africa was established, but the Caribbean was included only as a unit in the Managing Directorate for Latin America.

With these changes, aid was to become a much more explicit tool of EU foreign policy. The first indication of this came in a 2003 strategy paper by Javier Solana, the EU's High Representative for Common Foreign and Security Policy. The paper, 'A Secure Europe in a Better World', suggested that external assistance should support the EU's security agenda (Solana, 2003). For the Caribbean with little strategic significance, the paper's conclusions were a concern. More recent changes have aligned EU development policy with the Millennium Development Goals, which though important for African ACP countries are less significant for the Caribbean. The European Consensus on Development and the 'Global Europe' strategy (both from 2006), the 2009 Lisbon Treaty and the 2012 'Agenda for Change' placed greater focus on the eradication of poverty. Although an attempt was made in 2012 to re-emphasise the Caribbean–EU link via the Joint Caribbean–EU Partnership Strategy (Council of the European Union, 2012), this has done little to stem the tide away from the Caribbean. One consequence is a clear focus on differentiation, in other words '... graduating higher middle income countries from bilateral official development assistance ...' (Pape, 2013, p. 732). This was implemented from 2014 via the 11th European Development Fund (EDF). As Jessop (2013) argues, the '... policy is intended to place the future development emphasis on the world's poorest nations; move most development assistance for the Caribbean, other than Haiti, from national to regional support; and place its focus on issues such as the private sector, the environment, security and other cross cutting themes'.

Another reform that has undermined the EU's formerly close relations with the Caribbean is the enlargement of the EU. At the time of the signing of the first Lomé Convention, the EEC had nine member states. Today, the EU has 28 members—a large number of which are in Central and Eastern Europe and have little or no interest in the Caribbean. Also, the newer members have relatively high levels of poverty with wage levels and living standards far below the levels present in the states that were EU members prior to the 2004 enlargement. This means they are more conditioned to receive aid than to give it. As a result, there is little sympathy for, or understanding of, the challenges facing the Caribbean. This lack of interest is felt in all aspects of EU activity. There is now a majority of member states that have no historical ties to the ACP countries whatsoever, meaning that the balance within the EU has now shifted away from the ACP towards other geo-strategic interests. Also, even those members, such as the UK, with long-standing ties with the Caribbean are focusing their attention and resources elsewhere. As far back as 2004 Jessop argued: '[t]he Europe that the Caribbean has grown up with will cease. In its place will be a Union with a radically different relationship to the Caribbean and other relatively marginal regions of the world' (Jessop, 2004). This scenario has unfortunately come to pass.

THE COMMONWEALTH AND THE EUROPEAN UNION IN THE 21ST CENTURY

The Cotonou Agreement: The Last Hurrah?

The previous sections have highlighted how over time the relationship between the Caribbean and the EU has diminished. It was within this environment that a new agreement was needed to replace the fourth Lomé Convention, which had clearly run its course. Although the Cotonou Agreement incorporated commitments relating to political cooperation, trade and aid, many of the more progressive elements of Lomé were lost. Perhaps the most important pledge was that the 'ACP and the EU have agreed to conclude WTO-compatible trade agreements that will progressively remove barriers to trade between them and enhance cooperation in all areas relevant to trade' (European Commission, 2002, p. 6). The European Commission claimed that the planned EPAs were 'the way to help create a modern, twenty-first-century business environment, attract foreign direct investment, to grow markets and trade in order to reduce poverty' (CARICOM Secretariat, 2007). Negotiations for the EPA began in 2002 and it was signed in October 2008 between the EU and 14 CARICOM (Caribbean Community and Common Market) members plus the much larger and economically stronger Dominican Republic (known as CARIFORUM). Crucially, this was an agreement between the Caribbean and EU only, not the wider ACP grouping. It has been suggested that this 'shattered' long-standing ACP solidarity (Sanders, 2012a). This certainly weakened the Caribbean's negotiating position, although the importance of the ACP group should not be over-stated as its role had been in decline for some time (see Negre *et al.*, 2013).

The first priority of the negotiations between the Caribbean and EU, as indicated above, was to create an EPA that conformed to WTO rules, particularly to Articles XXIV of the GATT and V of the General Agreement on Trade in Services (GATS) that demand reciprocity and the liberalisation of 'substantially all' tariffs over a 'reasonable period of time'. However, both the EU and the Caribbean agreed to a degree of asymmetry in the application of the EPA. The EU committed to provide duty-free/quota-free (DFQF) market access to the EU for all CARIFORUM goods. Also, the DFQF market access under the EPA was now protected under WTO rules governing free trade areas, and this provided a degree of security for several traditional exports—although as we have seen the level of preference has since been undermined. For services, the EU agreed to liberalise 94% of its sector. The Caribbean for its part agreed that 87% of all goods from the EU would be liberalised by 2033, but that many revenue-sensitive products would not be liberalised. The transition period was agreed to give CARIFORUM time to find other revenue sources and for the region's industries to adjust to increased competition. For services, CARIFORUM agreed to open up 65–75% of its sector.

When the EPA was being negotiated and afterwards, there were considerable disagreements over its likely impact on the Caribbean. Those involved in the talks argued that the agreement would open up significant new export opportunities in goods and services for the Caribbean, improve competitiveness, and build regional markets. However, many academics and non-governmental organisations were critical. One critic suggested that the EU 'had "worked" a monumental deception on the region through a mixture of blatant bullyism, bribery, cajolery, deception, intellectual dishonesty and plain bluff' (Thomas, cited in Girvan, 2010, p. 92). For Girvan (2008, 2010), the EPA was in line with the EU's liberal global trade policy and would damage Caribbean interests. He claimed *inter alia* that: local companies would lose out to European companies in regional markets; governments would be unable to encourage the development of new national firms and cross-border production integration by regionally owned firms due to rules requiring equality of treatment with European companies; prospects in the EU services sector would be less than expected because of stringent eligibility criteria; Caribbean exports to the EU would still be limited by many non-tariff barriers; and FTAs negotiated by the EU would undermine the region's DFQF access.

Almost six years after the EPA was signed, some of the views of Girvan and other critics have perhaps been more prescient, but inaction and indifference have largely prevailed. Overall, implementation is progressing slowly. Only seven CARIFORUM states have ratified the EPA, and many have not yet implemented the necessary tariff reductions. The creation of EPA Implementation Units in each Caribbean country took longer than expected. All countries now have such a unit, but several are embedded within other government bodies and do not have sufficient money or staff to work effectively. Similarly, it has taken several years to establish the complex and costly set of institutions to oversee the agreement. In regard to trade flows, CARIFORUM service providers, a group that could benefit from the EPA, have been unable to access the EU market, while an increase in European goods and firms penetrating the Caribbean has not taken place. As Jessop (2012) suggested, 'very little that is practical has happened'. 'It is impossible to point to a single EPA specific success story … No one can point to any big investment or new trade flows'. Little has changed to challenge that view.

Several reasons can be offered to explain the problems noted above. (1) The aggressive way in which the EU undertook the negotiations has left a degree of bitterness and distrust on the Caribbean side, which has inhibited its engagement. As Bharrat Jagdeo, former prime minister of Guyana argued, the EPA is 'another instance of the European Union using its trade might and economic might bullying a developing country into an agreement' (BBC Caribbean.com, 2008). (2) A weakened and marginalised WTO undermined the intellectual rationale for the EPA (Heron, 2014). (3) Even though the EPA was sold as a development agreement there is little belief, on either side, that this will be the case. (4) Because the negotiations were largely an elite-driven process, the level of buy-in and commitment on the part of civil society and the private sector is small. In turn, they do not fully understand the agreement or believe it has much to offer them. As Jessop (2012) argued, '[m]any companies say it is an irrelevance'. Even the tourism sector 'has largely given up on the EPA' (Jessop, 2014). (5) The onset of the global economic crisis hit the Caribbean hard, which meant many states have been reluctant to move ahead with tariff reductions and lose much-needed revenue. (6) When governments have removed tariffs on EU goods, the early signs have been that 'a number of local companies have found themselves unable to compete' (Sanders, 2012b). Thus, this has created domestic pressures to slow down or even reverse the process of liberalisation. (7) Only limited resources have been provided by the EU to assist the Caribbean with implementing the EPA, and the process for accessing those funds has been 'cumbersome and bureaucratic' (Lindsay, 2013, p. 13). (8) Caribbean exporters continue to face non-tariff barriers in the EU market. (9) There is a view in Europe that the Caribbean is not an attractive trading partner owing to its lack of unity and widely different levels of development. As a consequence, these concerns and others have limited the impact of the EPA and raised new questions about the utility of maintaining the present model of Caribbean–EU relations in the future.

THE COMMONWEALTH AND THE EUROPEAN UNION IN THE 21ST CENTURY

The EU and the UK Overseas Territories

As was highlighted above when discussing the origins of the Lomé Convention, Part IV of the Treaty of Rome in 1957 first established links between the EU and the then colonies of some of its member states. Many of the colonies then became independent states and signed the Yaoundé and Lomé Conventions. However, a number of other territories did not move to independence and thus stayed under the provisions of Part IV, as Overseas Countries and Territories (OCTs). This status is still in place today, and there are 25 OCT countries linked to the UK, France, the Netherlands and Denmark. The UK has 11 OCTs spread across the globe, with five in the Caribbean; six if one includes Bermuda. These non-self-governing territories are not part of the EU and thus are not directly subject to EU law, but they are associate members of the EU. In the Treaty of Rome, the EEC's objectives to the OCT were: 'To promote the economic and social development of the countries and territories and to establish close economic relations between them and the Community as a whole' (Part IV, Article 131). The two fundamental elements of the relationship were 'the gradual freeing of trade between the associates and the EEC member states, and the provision of financial aid by member states to the associates through the European Development Fund' (Sutton, 2012, p. 106). Because of their shared origins, the OCT–EU relationship was in essence a 'light version' of the ACP–EU link, 'including more or less the same provisions' (Hannibal *et al.*, 2013, p. 80).

However, since 1991 when a new Association Decision was signed, OCT–EU relations have begun to diverge from the ACP–EU model. For example, as early as 1991, all OCT products were given free and unlimited access to the EU market, and in 1997 the OCTs were able to access a limited number of EU programmes '... on the grounds that many of the inhabitants of the OCT were citizens of the EU and therefore eligible to benefit from them' (Sutton, 2012, p. 108). Also, while the voice of Caribbean ACP countries was weakening in the EU, the influence of the OCTs was strengthening. For many years the OCTs had little say on the arrangements that affected them, but over the last decade they have been brought into the discussions. The OCTs now influence policy via structured dialogue with the EU, informal contacts, and the Overseas Countries and Territories Association, which recently established an office in Brussels. However, the OCTs '... continue to face restrictions on account of their non-sovereignty' (Sutton, 2012, p. 112), and in many cases the EU still plays second fiddle to the long-standing and dominant role of the administering powers.

In 2009 consultations began for a new Association Decision, and the European Commission stated that it was 'in favour of a significant change in the approach to the association of the OCTs with the EU' (Commission of the European Communities, 2009, p. 19). In particular, the Commission suggested that the new approach should recognise: (1) the OCTs as being part of the same 'European family' as the member states; and (2) their 'unique relationship' with the EU. After much debate a new agreement was adopted on 25 November 2013 (Council of the European Union, 2013). It aims to modernise the relationship between the OCTs and the EU, 'moving beyond development cooperation and focusing on a reciprocal relationship based on mutual interests'. A key provision is the creation of closer economic relations between the EU and the OCTs, such as through an improvement in market access for OCT goods and services, and relaxation of the rules of origin. Others include: enhancing the OCTs' competitiveness; strengthening their resilience and reducing their vulnerability; and creating more reciprocal relations between the EU and the OCTs based on mutual interests and shared values. There are also several financial instruments linked to the new Association Decision. Total EU funding for the OCTs via the 11th EDF is €364.5 million—a sizeable increase on the previous allocation. Two-thirds of that amount will be allocated to individual OCTs. In addition, they will receive funding under programmes by way of the EU's general budget.

The new Association Decision has been largely welcomed by the OCTs, and will provide an important additional level of support above and beyond the metropolitan powers. As Sutton argues, there '... is a shift of emphasis away from an Association Decision informed by EU relations with ACP countries towards one informed by the EU's commitment to its ORs (Outer-most Regions)'. (The ORs are integral but distant regions of EU member states.) Sutton continues, '[t]he EU's special relationship with the ACP has become more attenuated in recent years as the EU has at the same time invigorated its programmes with the ORs' (Sutton, 2012, p. 120). A key reason for this degree of convergence between the OCTs and ORs is that the arguments for assisting them are extremely similar: 'remoteness, insularity, smallness, climate, and economic dependence' (Sutton, 2012, p. 120). However, there will be limits to this convergence, mainly because the level of support from the EU to the ORs is very much higher than for the OCTs. Yet, as Hannibal *et al.* (2013, p. 90) argue, '[t]he OCTs have a unique position in Brussels, as they make up a peculiar category of colonial remnants maintaining a privileged position in the EU'.

A Broader Commonwealth Perspective

The article up to this point has concentrated on the relationship between the Caribbean and the EU, with occasional references to the supporting role of the ACP group. Of course, the Commonwealth incorporates the vast majority of ACP states and plays an important role in promoting the interests of small states in the international system. However, the Commonwealth's role in the changes that have been documented in this article has been relatively small. In particular, despite its advocacy on the particular vulnerabilities of small states, the organisation has been unable to change meaningfully the nature of global governance or the policy direction of the EU. Further, the ACP and CARIFORUM have been seen—for good reason—as the key interlocutors in relation to the EU, and therefore the Commonwealth has taken a back-seat. Indeed, perhaps the most tangible role has been through the Commonwealth Secretariat's management of the so-called 'Hub and Spokes' initiative (in collaboration with the ACP group, the Organisation Internationale de La Francophonie and the EU). The programme aims 'to enhance the capacity of key stakeholders in ACP countries to formulate suitable trade policy, participate effectively in international trade negotiations and implement international trade agreements' (The Commonwealth, 2014). The programme has been operating since 2004 and has had some successes, for example providing a range of briefs and position papers to help ACP officials conduct trade negotiations, and assisting St Vincent and the Grenadines in drafting its national trade policy. Although not inconsequential, such support has not changed the underlying dynamics of the Caribbean–EU relationship, and the fact that the EU is by far the largest funder of the programme is a

THE COMMONWEALTH AND THE EUROPEAN UNION IN THE 21ST CENTURY

concern in relation to its independence and effectiveness. In the words of a Brussels-based ACP representative, EU support means it is 'negotiating on both sides' (Jones and Weinhardt, 2015, p. 238). In comparison, the Commonwealth's role with the Overseas Territories is negligible because member countries are concerned about diluting the organisation's primary focus on independent states, and therefore little support is forthcoming for the non-sovereign territories.

Conclusion

It is clear that the nature of the relationship between the EU and the Caribbean, both for the independent Commonwealth states and for the non-independent territories, has changed greatly over the last two decades. Commonwealth Caribbean–EU relations have been undermined on two fronts: a diminution of the level of support provided by the EU both in relation to trade and aid and growing disenchantment on both sides about how the Cotonou Agreement and EPA are functioning. Since the first Lomé Convention, the Caribbean has been on the wrong side of dominant economic and trade-related narratives; but the region can also be criticised for not doing enough to build up its own diplomatic and economic position. Although the EPA will continue (largely because the EU is not offering a better alternative), the rationale for an ACP-wide post-Cotonou agreement is in doubt and it is difficult to see at the moment where the impetus will come for such a deal. For the EU, the Caribbean is a marginal interest, while the region is now exploring new opportunities with countries such as Brazil, China and Venezuela. Vestiges of the old relationship will remain, but the Caribbean will probably lose the final aspects of its particularism and will be subsumed into wider EU–Latin American structures—a process that has already begun. However, despite the antipathy on both sides, such a development sits uneasily with the Commonwealth Caribbean, because of their past strong links with the ACP. Ironically, it is the larger and more economically diverse Dominican Republic—a relative newcomer to the ACP group but also with strong links to Central America—that will benefit most from both the EPA and the EU's more general emphasis on Latin America. In relation to the UK OCTs, though starting from a similar place as the ACP states, have through their 'colonial' links with the UK become more closely intertwined with Europe. Being part of the EU, either directly or indirectly, has afforded a different approach to those outside the Union. For as long as the OCTs remain tied to their metropolitan powers their relatively close relationship with the EU will be assured. However, the OCTs are small in number and in size, and they will be unable—even if the desire was there—to help reboot or sustain the broader Commonwealth Caribbean–EU relationship.

References

ACP Press (2012) ACP preferences to erode as EU trade with third countries thrive, 30 October, http://www.acp.int/content/acp-preferences-erode-eu-trade-third-countries-thrive, accessed 15 June 2014.

Anania, G. (2010) *The Implications for Bananas of the Recent Trade Agreements between the EU and Andean and Central American Countries*, International Centre for Trade and Sustainable Development, Policy Brief 5, September, http://www.ictsd.org/themes/agriculture/the-implications-for-bananas-of-the-recent-trade-agreements-between-the-eu-and, accessed 14 June 2014.

THE COMMONWEALTH AND THE EUROPEAN UNION IN THE 21ST CENTURY

BBC Caribbean.com (2008) EPA: Caribbean still divided on treaty, 27 June, http://www.bbc.co.uk/caribbean/news/story/2008/06/080627_jagdeoepa.shtml, accessed 5 May 2015.

Cantore, N., Kennan, J. and Willem te Velde, D. (2012) *The Impact of EU Bilateral Trade Agreements with Third countries on the Caribbean Rum Sector.* London: Commonwealth Secretariat/Overseas Development Institute.

CARICOM Secretariat (2007) Press Release: CARIFORUM/EU EPA can be a world leader Georgetown, Guyana.

Commission of the European Communities (2009) Elements for a new partnership between the EU and the Overseas Countries and Territories (OCTs), Brussels, 6 November 2009 (COM), 2009 623 final.

Council of the European Union (2012) Council conclusions on the Joint Caribbean–EU Partnership Strategy, Brussels, 19 November, www.consilium.europa.eu/uedocs/cms_Data/docs/pressdata/EN/foraff/133566.pdf, accessed 18 August 2013.

Council of the European Union (2013) Council Decision 2013/755/EU of 25 November 2013 on the association of the overseas countries and territories with the European Union ('Overseas Association Decision'), *Official Journal of the European Union*, Brussels, 19 December 2003, L344/1.

Dunlop, A. (1999) What future for Lomé's commodity protocols?, ECDPM-CCE, June, ecdpm.org/.../DP-5-What-Future-For-Lomes-Commodity-Protocols-1999.pdf, accessed 20 June 2014.

European Commission (2002) *The Caribbean and the European Union.* Luxembourg: Office for the Official Publications of the European Communities.

Flint, A. (2008) *Trade, Poverty and the Environment: The EU, Cotonou and the African–Caribbean–Pacific Bloc.* Basingstoke: Palgrave Macmillan.

Girvan, N. (2008) Implications of the Cariforum–EC EPA, www.normangirvan.info/wp-content/uploads/2008/08/girvanimplicationsepa21jan.pdf, accessed 17 September 2009.

Girvan, N. (2010) Technification, sweetification, treatyfication: politics of the Caribbean–EU Economic Partnership Agreement, *Interventions—International Journal of Postcolonial Studies*, 12(1), pp. 100–111.

Gonzales, A. (1997) The future of the EU–Caribbean links, *The Courier*, 161, pp. 72–73.

Hadfield, A. (2007) Janus advances? An analysis of EC Development Policy and the 2005 amended Cotonou Partnership Agreement, *European Foreign Affairs Review*, 12, pp. 39–66.

Hannibal, I., Holst, K., Pram Gad, U. and Adler-Nissen, R. (2013) European Union: facilitating the OCTs in Brussels, in R. Adler-Nissen and U. Pram Gad (Eds), *European Integration and Postcolonial Sovereignty Games.* Oxford: Routledge.

Heron, T. (2014) Trading in development: norms and institutions in the making/unmaking of European Union-Africa, *Caribbean and Pacific trade and development cooperation, Contemporary Politics*, 20(1), pp. 10–22.

Holland, M. and Doidge, M. (2012) *Development Policy of the European Union.* Basingstoke: Palgrave Macmillan.

Jessop, D. (2004) *The Week in Europe, 2 April*, http://www.landofsixpeoples.com/news402/ns4040413.htm, accessed 5 May 2015. London: Caribbean Council of Europe.

Jessop, D. (2012) Can the EPA be made to work?, *The View from Europe*, 27 March, www.caribbean-council.org, accessed 28 March 2012.

Jessop, D. (2013) Europe's changing relationship with the Caribbean, *The View from Europe*, 17 May 2013, www.caribbean-council.org, accessed 18 May 2013.

Jessop, D. (2014) Should tourism give up on the EPA?, *The View from Europe*, 25 May 2014, www.caribbean-council.org, accessed 27 May 2013.

Jones, E. and Weinhardt, C. (2015) Echoes of colonialism in trade negotiations between the European Union and the African, Caribbean and Pacific countries, in K. Nicolaïdis, B. Sèbe and G. Maas (Eds.), *Echoes of Empire: Memory, Identity and Colonial Legacies.* London: I. B. Tauris.

Lindsay, C. (2013) The EU–CARIFORUM EPA: regulatory and policy changes and lessons for other ACP countries, *Caribbean Journal of International Relations and Diplomacy*, 1(3), pp. 5–29.

Negre, M., Keijzer, N., Lein, B. and Tissi, N. (2013) *Towards Renewal or Oblivion? Prospects for the Post-2020 Cooperation Between the European Union and the Africa, Caribbean and Pacific Group*, Discussion Paper 9/2013, German Development Institute, http://www.die-gdi.de/en/discussion-paper/article/towards-renewal-or-oblivion-prospects-for-post-2020-cooperation-between-the-european-union-and-the-africa-caribbean-and-pacific-group/, accessed 5 May 2015.

Pape, E. (2013) An old partnership in a new setting: ACP–EU relations from a European perspective, *Journal of International Development*, 25(5), pp. 727–741.

THE COMMONWEALTH AND THE EUROPEAN UNION IN THE 21ST CENTURY

Sanders, R. (2012a) Cutting EU aid should be resisted, but begging bowl not enough, 7 September, http://www.sirronaldsanders.com/viewarticle.aspx?ID=328, accessed 8 September 2012.

Sanders, R. (2012b) Tenth anniversary of the EPA negotiations: not a time for celebration, 3 October, http://www.sirronaldsanders.com/viewarticle.aspx?ID=331, accessed 5 October 2012.

Solana, J. (2003) A Secure Europe in a Better World, Brussels, 12 December.

Sutton, P. (2012) The European Union and its Overseas Counties and Territories: the search for a new relationship, in P. Clegg and D. Killingray (Eds.), *The Non-Independent Territories of the Caribbean and Pacific: Continuity or Change?* London: Institute of Commonwealth Studies.

The Commonwealth (2014) Supporting countries to reap the benefits of international trade: Hub & Spokes, http://thecommonwealth.org/project/supporting-countries-reap-benefits-international-trade-hub-spokes, accessed 5 May 2015.

The Courier, Journal of ACP and EU Affairs (1975) ACP–EEC Convention of Lomé, special issue, 31, March, Commission of the European Communities.

The Daily Herald (2015) ACP countries alarmed at collapse in sugar prices, 10 April, http://www.thedailyher ald.com/index.php?option=com_content&view=article&id=54756:acp-countries-alarmed-at-collapse-in-sugar-prices&catid=2:news&Itemid=5, accessed 2 May 2015.

Woolcock, S. (2007) *European Union Policy towards Free Trade Agreements*, Working Paper No. 3, European Centre for International Political Economy, http://www.ecipe.org/publications/european-union-policy-to wards-free-trade-agreements/, accessed 14 June 2014.

International Organisations and the Evolution of Humanitarianism: Cross-perspectives on the Commonwealth and the European Union

LOLA WILHELM
Graduate Institute of International and Development Studies, Geneva, Switzerland

ABSTRACT   *As international relations actors in the post-Second World War world, international organisations have played a significant role in the standardisation of global policy concepts during the 20th century, and humanitarian assistance has been no exception. While the study of the role of international organisations in shaping a dominant model of humanitarian aid has recently gathered pace, few historians have focused on different, less successful models and interpretations developed by other international organisations. Recently declassified Commonwealth Secretariat records show that discussions within the Secretariat and among member states regarding the potential objectives and scope of Commonwealth humanitarian assistance programmes took place as early as the 1960s, and continued throughout the following decades. This article provides an overview of the origin and evolution of the Commonwealth's approach to humanitarian assistance since the 1960s. Its objective is to document this hitherto little known aspect of Commonwealth assistance policies, and, based on an initial literature and archival survey, to contribute to the identification of further research questions and gaps in this aspect of Commonwealth history. Although they are very different in nature and scope, the Commonwealth and the European Union share at least one common feature in so far as humanitarian assistance is concerned, namely their difficulty in reaching a consensual definition of it. By exploring the links and discrepancies between, as well as within, each organisation's approach to humanitarian assistance, and by examining the initiatives of some of their member states, this paper seeks to highlight the plasticity of the definition of humanitarian assistance.*

Introduction

At the Malta Commonwealth Heads of Governments Meeting (CHOGM) in November 2005, Commonwealth member states tasked the Secretary-General with developing a mechanism for 'establishing and operationalising' the proposed 'Commonwealth Programme for Natural Disaster Management', with the aim of fostering cooperation between member states for 'capacity building for disaster risk reduction and disaster response management'.[1] What motivated this decision was a concern with 'the devastating and increasing impact of natural and man-made disaster on human lives, infrastructures and economies'.[2] Member states also pledged to 'support efforts to further strengthen the international humanitarian response system, including the proposed extension of the UN Central Emergency Revolving Fund and the strengthening of the UN humanitarian coordination'.[3] A few months earlier, the United Nations had launched an ambitious plan to reorganise the global humanitarian system, the Humanitarian Reform process, following a study commissioned by the Under-Secretary-General for Humanitarian Affairs and Emergency Relief Coordinator (USG-ERC), the head of the UN Office for the Coordination of Humanitarian Affairs (OCHA) (Adinolfi *et al.*, 2005).

Considering the Commonwealth's usually narrow focus on specific development issues and on democracy and human rights promotion on the one hand, and its limited resources in comparison with larger international organisations on the other, its involvement in humanitarian assistance may appear as a historical oddity. Yet, recently declassified Commonwealth Secretariat records show that discussions within the Secretariat and among member states regarding the potential objectives and scope of Commonwealth humanitarian assistance programmes took place as early as the 1960s, and continued throughout the following decades. This development followed the establishment of the Commonwealth Secretariat in 1965, an event commonly viewed as reflecting the modernisation of the organisation.

As actors of international relations on the post-Second World War world scene, international organisations have played a significant role in the standardisation of global policy concepts during the 20th century, and humanitarian assistance has been no exception.[4] In the last decade, studies have investigated the role of the League of Nations, the United Nations, and, more recently, of regional organisations such as the European Union, in shaping a dominant model of humanitarian aid.[5] However, few historians have focused on different, less successful models and on interpretations developed by other international organisations. Coincidentally, this question has been largely neglected by Commonwealth studies and Commonwealth historiography. It is this double gap in the literature that this paper seeks to address through a case study of Commonwealth approaches to humanitarian aid.

The examination of the organisation's humanitarian programmes reveals that the actual scale of Commonwealth humanitarian assistance has been modest, to the point of appearing somewhat tokenistic. However, the Commonwealth's apparent compliance with humanitarian agendas set by larger players since the 1990s, such as the European Union, conceals a more nuanced historical evolution. The objective of this article is therefore primarily to document this hitherto little known aspect of Commonwealth assistance policies, and, based on an exploratory survey of the literature and archives on the subject, to contribute to the identification of further research on this aspect of Commonwealth history. Although they are very different in nature and scope, the Commonwealth and the European Union share at least one common feature in so far as humanitarian assistance is concerned, namely their difficulty in trying to reach a consensual definition of it. By exploring the links and discrepancies between, as well as within, each organisation's approach to humanitarian assistance, and by examining the initiatives of some of their member states, this paper seeks to highlight the plasticity of the definition of humanitarian assistance.

Considering the Commonwealth's tentative participation in humanitarian assistance from the 1960s onwards, how have Commonwealth approaches to humanitarian assistance since 1965 compared with those of other international organisations such as the United Nations and the European Community/Union, and with broader trends within the humanitarian system? Has this tentative model been marginal, or has it contributed to highlighting gaps in this system? The examination of relevant Commonwealth Secretariat records and open official documents provides a number of answers to these questions and highlights the need for further scholarly interest in these topics.

First, this paper considers the complex definition of humanitarianism and assesses how significant evolutions in the humanitarian system from the 1960s to the late 1980s provided opportunities and incentives for international organisations to become increasingly involved in humanitarian initiatives. It then discusses Commonwealth involvement in humanitarian aid before the 1990s, and the potential impact of this involvement for the broader history of humanitarianism. The subsequent section examines evolutions within the humanitarian system and within international organisations from the 1990s onwards, focusing on specific Commonwealth and EU case studies. By so doing, I seek to highlight commonalities and discrepancies between Commonwealth perceptions and the broader humanitarian system, and the specificities of Commonwealth views during subsequent stages of humanitarian history. I shall also highlight the variety of approaches and interpretations that coexisted within the organisations themselves, including among member states and Secretariats.

Humanitarian Assistance: A Historiographical Discussion

The very definition of humanitarian assistance, or, as a number of political scientists and historians put it, humanitarianism, is the subject of ongoing scholarly discussions. Until recently, research on humanitarianism had been the preserve of political science and sociology, and had tended to focus on the institutional frameworks of specific international organisations, as well as on their moral and ethical underpinnings.[6] Although historical research on the topic started gathering pace a decade ago, attempts at connecting these within a wider, *longue-durée* framework remain scarce.[7] The more recent historiography has thus tended to liken the history of humanitarian assistance to a patchwork of heterogeneous, overlapping, loosely interconnected trends rather than to a coherent movement.[8] In this context, determining what constitutes, or qualifies as, humanitarian assistance at different stages of history remains a tentative process. As Michael Barnett and Thomas G. Weiss have noted, it may range from any act 'intended to save lives and reduce suffering' to 'the impartial, independent, and neutral provision of relief to those in immediate need because of conflict and natural disasters' (Barnett and Weiss, 2008, p. 5).

Historians have argued that the 18th century abolitionist movement constituted an early manifestation of humanitarianism, thereby highlighting the importance of various philanthropic, religious and missionary groups in the development of the movement's moral and cultural framework (Haskell, 1985).[9] The period from the late 19th century to the Second World War is commonly presented as a stage of haphazard consolidation of this nascent humanitarian system.

The first Convention for the Amelioration of the Condition of the Wounded in Armies in the Field (1864) constituted one of its earliest official frameworks. Its signatories agreed that 'ambulances and military hospitals shall be recognized as neutral, and as such, protected and respected by the belligerents as long as they accommodate wounded and sick'.[10] Having undergone multiple revisions throughout the first half of the 20th century, the 1949 Geneva Convention, as it became known, still constitutes the main pillar of humanitarian law today.

The explicit recognition of non-governmental organisations (NGOs) as major humanitarian relief players, such as the Red Cross, which was founded in Geneva in 1863, was an inherent component of the rise of this state-endorsed legal humanitarian framework.[11] One obvious limitation of this legal definition, however, was that it restricted the concept of humanitarian assistance to the context of armed conflicts. However, from the late 19th century onward, humanitarian responders were also active in the aftermath of natural disasters (Hutchinson, 2000, pp. 4, 9).

The devastation of the First World War and the famines that stemmed from it provided a fertile ground for the development of a culture of humanitarianism in the inter-war period, leading to the establishment of new charitable organisations, such as the Save the Children Fund, which was founded in the United Kingdom in 1919 (Chabbott, 1999; Mendlesohn, 1999; Barnett, 2011, pp. 83–85). The movement was, at that point, still rooted in the paternalistic, imperialistic tradition of earlier forms of humanitarianism; it was also, however, influenced by the epoch's faith in scientific progress and techniques (Mendlesohn, 1999, p. 10).[12] The Second World War accelerated the specialisation of the humanitarian sector. From 1945 to 1990, as European colonial empires were dismantled and the geographical focus of humanitarianism moved away from post-war Europe to the Third World, this phase of the movement's history culminated with the affirmation of a standardised, apolitical model of humanitarian assistance between 1980 and 1990 (Barnett, 2011, p. 2).[13] Although the historiography on the topic is virtually non-existent, the question of pre- and post-disaster assistance as additional components of humanitarian assistance seems, on the whole, to have come to prominence during this period.[14]

By contrast, the post-Cold War era has been portrayed as a phase of redefinition of humanitarian aid, when foreign military interventions and humanitarian aid have constituted two sides of the same coin. In Michael Barnett's own, ironic words:

> In the 1990s, everything changed. The Cold War was history, replaced by 'new wars' that were creating 'complex humanitarian emergencies'. In fact, these wars were not so new, and humanitarian emergencies had always been complex, but the international community acted as if they had never seen anything like them ... The humanitarian community did not completely meet these challenges ... but did expand dramatically in scope and scale and provided new forms of assistance to more people than ever before. (Barnett, 2011, pp. 2–3)

Although this dichotomy has been, and must be, nuanced, including through an analysis of the continuities between these two phases, it seems a valid framework when looking more specifically at humanitarian aid in international organisations.

Just like the literature on humanitarianism in general, the sub-topic of the creation of international organisations dedicated to humanitarian aid, or the establishment of humanitarian aid mechanisms within existing international organisations, has tended to be examined primarily through the theoretical frameworks of political science.[15] While some historians have developed useful analyses of multilateral humanitarian assistance mechanisms over the longer term, efforts to cover the second half of the 20th century remain scarce, and tend to be excessively dependent on institutional accounts.[16]

The creation of humanitarian agencies within international organisations in the early 1990s constituted a significant step in the institutionalisation of the humanitarian aid system. In 1992, the United Nations General Assembly established the Department of Humanitarian Affairs (DHA) under the United Nations Secretariat (Steets et al., 2012; United Nations, 1991), and the European Community Humanitarian Office (ECHO) was created the same year (European Commission, 1991). Although no equivalent landmark can be found in Commonwealth history, the organisation also attempted to develop a coherent approach to the question of humanitarian assistance, particularly from the 1990s onwards. This display of common humanitarian principles and objectives within international organisations, however, also concealed internal discrepancies. As this paper will discuss below, Britain, as a member of the European Union and the Commonwealth, has occasionally criticised the humanitarian policies of both organisations.

The tendency of the humanitarian sector to become both more professionalised (Siméant and Dauvin, 2004) but also, crucially, more institutionalised, in fact pre-dated the turn of the 1990s. In terms of external factors, the political context of the Cold War and decolonisation had seemed to vindicate the Geneva Convention's long-held premise that neutral humanitarian organisations were particularly well-equipped to access victims in conflict zones. Whereas until the end of the Second World War and in its immediate aftermath humanitarian responders had been guided by diverse world views and ethical principles, from the 1960s onward, humanitarian organisations started adopting the principles of humanity, neutrality and impartiality as the core values of humanitarianism (Barnett, 2011, p. 6). In terms of public relations, the rapid expansion of a set of standardised humanitarian principles served the double purpose of securing private donations and of influencing the foreign policy of Western governments through the denunciation of war crimes and genocides (Dauvin, 2010, pp. 7–13).

How did this evolution affect the realm of international organisations? Few historical studies have focused on the development of humanitarian policies within international organisations beyond the interwar and Second World War work of the League of Nations, the Red Cross and the United Nations. Based on the broader historiography on the aid and development record of international organisations in the post-Second World War period, it appears that at least two elements have to be taken into account in order to answer this question. First, in the early 1960s, the international organisations scene was deeply influenced by the new membership of formerly colonised states, by the geopolitical alliances of the Cold War, and by the rise of the Third World movement. Second, although aid was generally considered as a highly political issue, the aid agendas of the Eastern, Western and Non-Aligned blocks alike were almost invariably dominated by concerns for development and modernisation rather than humanitarian aid.

In addition, the purposes of humanitarian assistance remained disputed within international organisations. The Commonwealth's original interpretation of humanitarian assistance, which was closely linked to the Rhodesian Unilateral Declaration of Independence (UDI) crisis (1965–80), was often at odds with British views on the matter. Meanwhile, the European Community's mention of foreign humanitarian aid, although it dated back a 1970s convention, was embedded within a primarily development-oriented technical and financial assistance agenda with the African, Caribbean and Pacific (ACP) countries. This partly explains why a budding humanitarian universalism only belatedly penetrated international organisations.

Early attempts at creating intergovernmental humanitarian organisations had occurred under the auspices of the League of Nations, leading to the short-lived Office of the High Commissioner for Refugees (1921) and International Relief Union (1927). During and after the Second World War, a number of specialised agencies of the United Nations were given a mandate by the General Assembly to address narrowly defined humanitarian issues as part of broader aid portfolios, such as the United Nations Relief and Rehabilitation Agency (UNRRA), the United Nations High Commissioner for Refugees (UNHCR) (1950) and the World Food Programme (1961). This phase produced mixed results, and resulted in an unsystematic coverage of humanitarian crises, which partly motivated the creation of the Office of the United Nations Disaster Relief Coordinator (UNDRO) in 1971. UNDRO was specifically in charge of coordinating the humanitarian efforts of the United Nations; however, its mandate applied to natural disasters only. Member states therefore appear to have kept the more controversial topic of humanitarian relief to conflict-affected areas out of the purview of this new, dedicated humanitarian agency (Fromuth, 1988, p. 177); although research into the position of key UN member states is ongoing, conclusions are yet to be made available.[17]

By keeping politically sensitive issues at arm's length, the United Nations, therefore, endorsed an interpretation of humanitarian aid that predominated over the period— namely, that humanitarianism did not belong in state-dominated organisations. However, Michael Barnett has challenged the idea that humanitarian NGOs were ever successful in distancing themselves from political agendas during this period. Conversely, the activity of the Commonwealth of Nations tends to support the idea that decision-makers within intergovernmental organisations did not necessarily see humanitarian assistance as prohibited territory before 1990.

The New Commonwealth and Humanitarian Concerns: The Southern African Connection

Between 1945 and 1965, the Commonwealth of Nations evolved from a still largely Anglo-centric, imperial 'club' to an increasingly multilateral organisation (McIntyre, 2001, p. 693). This transitional phase was marked by several internal crises, such as India's application for continued Commonwealth membership as a republic (1949) and the criticism by several member states of London's handling of the Suez crisis (1956), which eroded Britain's organisational leverage (Orde, 1996, p. 183). By the early 1960s, the disillusionment of British foreign policy-makers with the Commonwealth was matched by repeated but unsuccessful attempts at reinforcing the United Kingdom's economic and political ties with the European Economic Community, and by changes in the United Kingdom's Commonwealth immigration policy through a series of restrictive measures (Butler, 2002; Darwin, 1988). In 1965, the Commonwealth's increasing emancipation from London was marked by the creation of the Commonwealth Secretariat. This was shortly followed by a crisis that further crystallised diplomatic tensions among Commonwealth members, as the UDI by Southern Rhodesia's white minority regime threw the organisation into turmoil.

THE COMMONWEALTH AND THE EUROPEAN UNION IN THE 21ST CENTURY

Commonwealth involvement in humanitarian assistance may appear as somewhat accidental. Yet, inconsistent as it may appear with the emphasis put on development and democracy-promotion in its 1971 Singapore declaration, it provides a useful illustration of the diversity of organisational views regarding humanitarianism during the post-Second World War period. A retrospective analysis seems to suggest that the Commonwealth Secretariat contributed unintentionally to the creation of the institutional space within which humanitarian programmes were discussed by Commonwealth states. One of the outcomes of the 1966 Commonwealth Prime Ministers' Meeting in Lagos, which took place at the height of the dispute between the United Kingdom and the African members of the Commonwealth over British Prime Minister Harold Wilson's refusal to use force against the Smith regime (Smith, 1981; Roiron, 2013), was the creation of a Commonwealth Sanctions Committee tasked with monitoring the enforcement by Commonwealth member states of the international sanctions imposed by the UN Security Council against the UDI regime, and to make recommendations to improve their effectiveness.[18] From 1973 onward, the Committee became one of the main multilateral forums for the discussion of Commonwealth assistance to Southern African nationalists.[19]

One of the earliest mentions of humanitarian aid in a public Commonwealth document can be found in the final communiqué of the 1973 CHOGM in Ottawa:

> Heads of Government reviewed the efforts of the indigenous people of the territories of Southern Africa to achieve self-determination and independence and agreed on the need to give any humanitarian assistance to all those engaged in such efforts.[20]

Britain, it should be noted, expressed reservations vis-à-vis such assistance, on the grounds that it might be diverted for military purposes.[21] The CHOGM's politicised interpretation of humanitarian assistance was not outlandish in the context of the early 1970s: within the NGO sector, discursive paradoxes had arisen between the need to uphold humanitarian neutrality on the one hand, and the 'duty to testify' against human rights and humanitarian law violations on the other (Dauvin, 2010, p. 13).

In terms of structure, the Secretariat's humanitarian assistance programmes initially referred merely to existing programmes, such as the Commonwealth Programme for Rhodesians, which had been created at the Lagos meeting.[22] Following the 1971 Summit in Singapore, the management of most of these programmes was transferred to the Commonwealth Fund for Technical Cooperation (CFTC), which played a role in the shaping of Commonwealth diplomacy, under the supervision of the Secretariat.[23] Other CFTC interventions in the Rhodesian crisis included financial support to Zambia when the country decided to impose an embargo on all economic exchanges with Rhodesia in 1973.[24] In 1976, the Commonwealth Secretariat accepted a UN Secretariat request for the secondment of a CFTC expert to the UN Sanctions Committee, which dealt with sanctions against discriminatory regimes.[25] Commonwealth heads of governments later pledged to extend their humanitarian assistance to Mozambique via the Commonwealth Fund for Mozambique, a decision taken at the 1975 CHOGM in Kingston following behind-the-scenes discussions between the Secretariat and FRELIMO (Smith, 1981, pp. 221–223).[26]

THE COMMONWEALTH AND THE EUROPEAN UNION IN THE 21ST CENTURY

In terms of scale, data on the actual resources of these programmes is patchy, and does not at this stage permit an in-depth analysis of their significance, beyond their symbolic value. For instance, although it remains difficult to ascertain the scope of the actual contributions of Commonwealth member states, India and Tanzania pledged, respectively, 900,000 rupees and 200,000 Tanzanian shillings to the Commonwealth Fund for Mozambique in 1977.[27] In terms of their nature, however, the records reveal a focus on scholarship and 'manpower training' programmes, which constituted the main model of Commonwealth humanitarian assistance to Southern Africa throughout the 1970s.[28]

Commonwealth Secretariat records, it should be noted, provide only a partial account of the organisation's perception of the objectives of humanitarian assistance at the time. Just as the Secretariat viewed humanitarian assistance as a way of advancing a political agenda in Southern Africa, other member states also tended to view such aid as a geopolitical tool. However, their objectives could sometimes be quite different from those of the Secretariat in the context of the Cold War. Two examples in particular may help highlight the discrepancies between the Secretariat's programmes, which were primarily concerned with the Southern African crises, and the humanitarian agendas of some Commonwealth member states, for whom humanitarian assistance was part of a broader Cold War context. The Canadian government, for instance, is recorded to have used the Colombo Plan, a post-war regional development initiative born from a Commonwealth meeting in 1950, to channel its humanitarian assistance to South Vietnam, as a token of its non-military support to the United States, despite the country's declared neutrality.[29] Some member states, meanwhile, distanced themselves from the Commonwealth Secretariat's approach to humanitarian assistance because it challenged their foreign policy agendas—Britain, for instance, was sceptical of Commonwealth assistance to African nationalists throughout the 1970s, on the grounds that it might fuel terrorism.

Commonwealth undertakings from 1965 to 1990 therefore seemed to reflect two contradictory trends that characterised the evolution of the humanitarian movement at the time: the affirmation of humanitarianism as an apolitical cause on the one hand, and the duty of humanitarianism to denounce oppressive regimes in a highly antagonised Cold War context on the other hand. By privileging a militant definition of humanitarian assistance in the context of Southern African and the geopolitical crises of the Cold War, Commonwealth member states, with the support of the Secretariat and despite their internal divisions, seem to have adopted a less consensual definition than the United Nations. Yet, the Commonwealth's use of humanitarianism as a label intended to legitimise assistance to African nationalists also reflected the trans-partisan credentials of the concept, since it seemed to be used primarily to avoid a potential veto by London. Limited as this interest—and its practical implementation—may have been, it was aligned with the contemporary interpretations, and contradictions, of humanitarian assistance.

The extent to which humanitarian assistance simply constituted a bargaining chip in Commonwealth discussions, or translated into actual programmes, remains difficult to ascertain, and would benefit from further archival research, including into the archives of relevant member states. The next section shows that, by contrast, the Commonwealth's subsequent humanitarian endeavours became increasingly technical and specialised, arguably replicating broader evolutions of humanitarianism.

Bridging the Humanitarian–Development Divide?

Just as institutionalisation has been presented as one of the main characteristics of the evolution of the humanitarian sector from 1945 to 1990, the following phase has frequently been associated with a qualitative and quantitative expansion of the realm of humanitarian assistance. On a macroscopic scale, according to a widespread historical narrative, this was reflected by at least two tidal changes in the humanitarian aid sector.

First, as part of major foreign assistance reorientations, official humanitarian aid funding started to grow exponentially in the 1990s.[30] Second, partly as a result of their new-found economic momentum, and partly due to the end of tacit Cold War embargos on foreign assistance, humanitarian actors intervened in ever larger emergencies, such as the Iraqi Kurd refugee crisis (1991), the Rwandan genocide (1994) and the conflicts in the former Republic of Yugoslavia. In exchange for their donors' financial generosity, humanitarian agencies—international organisations included—also faced strong expectations that this should lead to a qualitative growth of their portfolio of activities, including crisis preparedness and prevention, and post-crisis recovery.[31] This generosity, it could be added, was short-lived, as from the mid-2000s humanitarian organisations came under scrutiny and financial pressure from their donors.

Some NGO executives viewed the increased weight of state-funded humanitarian aid, and the implied reduction of humanitarian aid to a development issue, as a threat to their impartiality.[32] Some academics, however, have objected that the impartiality of the NGO sector was never as robust as this argument would imply, and, conversely, that state participation in humanitarian assistance mechanisms was not an unprecedented phenomenon—and as the earlier section of this paper discussed, was in fact one of its founding features (Barnett, 2011, p. 5).

Unsurprisingly perhaps, the scholarship on the involvement of international organisations in the humanitarian sector still appears to grapple with the dialectical tension between two apparently diverging trends: the assumed politicisation of the sector, through its institutional intertwining with development aid; and its increasingly technical and neutral veneer. As mentioned above, 1992 was a landmark for the institutionalisation of humanitarian aid, with the creation of ECHO and the UN DHA (later renamed OCHA). The creation of humanitarian coordination agencies was justified by the failure of existing multilateral humanitarian mechanisms to address humanitarian crises, but also by the need for better institutional responses to the increasing scale and complexity of these humanitarian crises (Cox, 2009; Steets *et al.*, 2012).

Whereas their role had previously been discrete, international organisations, as the repositories of the collective agendas of their member states but also as bureaucracies, acted as catalysts of this transition. The evolution of one of the main multilateral actors of humanitarian aid, the European Community, showed the ambivalence of this pivotal phase of humanitarian assistance.

With contributions averaging around one billion euros annually since the late 1990s, the European Union has constituted one of the largest humanitarian donors globally (Versluys, 2009, p. 93). As development aid became more political after 1990, by contrast, 'the apolitical nature of ECHO has been constantly emphasised' (Stewart, 2006, p. 113). This claim has since been substantiated by the first reference to humanitarian assistance in a European Union treaty in 2009, which affirmed that 'humanitarian aid

THE COMMONWEALTH AND THE EUROPEAN UNION IN THE 21ST CENTURY

operations shall be conducted in compliance with the principles ... of impartiality, neutrality and non-discrimination'.[33]

This analysis suggests that with ECHO, the European Union departed from a previously politicised model of humanitarian aid. Humanitarian aid had first been included as a component of European external assistance in the Second Yaoundé Convention (1969–75), which set the terms of trade and economic relations between the European Economic Community and the Associated Countries.[34] Until 1992, its implementation was managed by several European Commission Directorate-Generals on an ad hoc basis, with DG-Development considered by at least one scholar as its foremost implementing body (Versluys, 2009; Sicurelli, 2013, p. 37).

But while the literature does recognise that Europe's humanitarian aid was indeed associated with a broader development agenda, whether the developments of 1992 actually reversed this trend remains the object of debate. The European Union's humanitarian programmes are thus still described as '"symbolic politics" ... allowing the Union to assert its identity ... on the international scene', and aimed at '[consolidating] the loyalty of European citizens towards European integration' in a post-Cold War world (Versluys, 2009, p. 91).

Although some scholars believe that the venture into the politicised realms of conflict-resolution and development issues was a short-lived phase of ECHO's existence, the articulation between humanitarian aid and development remained a priority for international organisations, as the European Commission's 2001 guidelines on 'Linking Relief, Rehabilitation, and Development' and the 2005 UN World Conference on Disaster Reduction indicated (Versluys, 2013, p. 93). By the mid-2000s, disaster preparedness and disaster recovery were broadly recognised as components of humanitarian assistance.

The decision to create a European humanitarian office in 1992, it has been argued, concealed some internal divisions between member states (Cox, 2009). A deeper investigation of Britain's role in this development would provide a meaningful illustration of the similarities between the Commonwealth's and the European Union's difficulties in the field of humanitarian assistance. Britain, as discussed previously, had not been a fervent supporter of the Commonwealth's humanitarian policies. Its admission into the European Community, in 1973, had been viewed as evidence of its wavering bonds with the Commonwealth.[35] However, and although more evidence would be required to buttress this hypothesis, this reorientation did not appear to alter fundamentally its cool attitude towards multilateral humanitarian mechanisms. Rather than supporting the European Community's humanitarian initiative in the early 1990s, Britain has thus been reported to have discreetly supported its opponents, first and foremost the NGO sector, on the grounds that such a scheme duplicated and, possibly, competed with existing national policies.[36]

Similar tensions could be observed in the evolution of the Commonwealth's approach to humanitarian assistance over the same period, both in terms of its definition of humanitarianism and in terms of its institutional structure and programmes.

As the analysis of the Commonwealth's involvement in Southern African crises demonstrated, the organisation never appeared to consider humanitarian assistance as a separate set of policies, but rather as a mostly symbolic instrument for the pursuit of its political objectives—the termination of segregationist regimes. As this chapter of history came to a close, it would not have been entirely surprising if the humanitarian theme had disappeared from the organisation's list of concerns altogether. Yet, although archival sources are not available for this period, the official literature indicates that this was not the case. Rather, the Commonwealth, like other international organisations, seems to have progressively treated humanitarian assistance as a distinct set of policies, and to have separated them from its political activities.

In terms of political mandate, the Commonwealth has built its reputation as a consensus-based, non-coercive organisation to promote the principles of human rights and democracy affirmed in its 1991 Harare Declaration, through the creation of dedicated mechanisms.[37] One such mechanism was the Commonwealth Ministerial Action Group, a high-level group established in 1995 to provide good offices for peace and pre-emptive diplomacy, and to promote democracy across the organisation. The suspension of Commonwealth member states from the organisation on the grounds of their systematic violations of the Harare principles constitutes a further example of the organisation's human rights advocacy work; however, it also insists on the conciliatory nature of Commonwealth interventions.[38]

In parallel, the Commonwealth has repeatedly tried to establish a dedicated humanitarian assistance scheme. The first of such attempts occurred in the aftermath of the 1995 CHOGM in Auckland, when Commonwealth leaders asked the Secretariat to take 'follow-up measures' in order to implement the recommendations of the Report of the Intergovernmental Group on the Emergence of a Global Humanitarian Order, 'Towards a More Humane World'.[39] However, the drivers and motivations behind this initiative are unclear, and its achievements, if any, remain undocumented. A decade later, large-scale natural disasters such as the 2004 Indian Ocean tsunami and the 2005 Pakistan earthquake fostered a sense of renewed urgency among member states, leading to a proposal for a Commonwealth Programme for Natural Disaster Management at the 2005 Malta CHOGM.[40]

By then, Commonwealth Secretariat staff seemed aware of the organisation's limited ability to respond to humanitarian crises in the traditional sense, even though the Secretariat stated that it had 'responded to requests for assistance by member Governments' in the aftermath of natural disasters in Pakistan, the Maldives, Grenada and Guyana.[41] They had, however, taken stock of the emergence of disaster risk reduction as a new field of humanitarian assistance. Therefore, despite the limited success of past Commonwealth humanitarian assistance projects, the Secretariat did dedicate some of its Governance and Institutional Development Division's expertise and, possibly, resources to disaster risk reduction capacity-building programmes. Nevertheless, the sustainability of such projects remains uncertain, considering recent financial setbacks of the Commonwealth Secretariat.[42]

Since 1990, Commonwealth humanitarian assistance has assimilated innovations within the humanitarian aid system, including the creation of dedicated, specialised entities to manage humanitarian aid separately from other types of assistance, and the inclusion of pre- and post-disaster assistance as components of humanitarian aid. However, it has also mirrored the continuing ambivalence of the concept's definition, by abstaining from establishing a clear distinction between security-related and humanitarian agendas. Arguably, references to the 'security, humanitarian and development dimensions'[43] of small arms proliferation and to the 'humanitarian crisis caused by anti-personnel mines'[44] in CHOGM final communiqués recognise that humanitarian issues have been considered, if only rhetorically, as part of a more global set of security and

THE COMMONWEALTH AND THE EUROPEAN UNION IN THE 21ST CENTURY

development issues. Interestingly, this approach does not seem entirely inconsistent with that of one of the Commonwealth's most active member states, namely the United Kingdom. British and other Western humanitarian programmes in Afghanistan, for instance, have routinely been presented as part and parcel of a broader, civil and military attempt at re-establishing and maintaining peace, democracy and security not only in the country of intervention, but also at home, despite the reluctance of the non-governmental sector to adhere to this agenda.[45]

Conclusion

This survey has demonstrated that over the studied period, Commonwealth engagement with humanitarian assistance has shifted from its original opposition to oppressive regimes to a focus on issues of preparedness in the face of natural disasters. Yet, despite this apparent contrast, little change has occurred as far as the methods of this humanitarian assistance—capacity-building—are concerned. Overall, this evolution and the continued ambivalence of the organisation's perception of humanitarian assistance have followed the sweeping reorganisation of the aid sector, which the European Union and the United Nations helped crystallise. A common feature of European and Commonwealth policies regarding humanitarian assistance has indeed been their hesitation between a more neutral, disaster relief-oriented definition of humanitarian aid and a more holistic but also less neutral definition that includes disaster preparedness and recovery dimensions, as well as security concerns.

Although British views could have appeared, at least for a while, as compatible with the European Union's post-1990 humanitarian assistance agenda, European aid mechanisms have been routinely criticised by British aid officials, alongside other multilateral aid systems, such as the Commonwealth.[46]

The scholarship on humanitarian aid in international organisations after 1945 has revolved around the dichotomy between development aid as a political tool and humanitarian assistance as an apolitical one; or, in other words, the varying politicisation of humanitarian assistance through the different phases of its history. As Commonwealth humanitarian assistance has indicated, this analytical framework tends to overlook a wider variety of political and operational constraints within international organisations. A more detailed, systematic analysis of the internal debates and tensions within international organisations as well as between them may help to produce a more nuanced understanding of the significance of this phenomenon. With a view to encouraging such research, this paper has explored a possible comparative framework for the study of humanitarian assistance in international organisations since 1945, and highlighted the value that case studies of less frequently studied players, such as the Commonwealth, may bring to such historical political surveys.

Notes

1. 'The Malta Communiqué (2005) Final Communiqué from the Commonwealth Heads of Government Meeting (CHOGM) in Malta, 25–27 November 2005, http://assets.thecommonwealth.org/assetbank-commonwealth/action/viewAsset?id=19556&index=11&total=1000&categoryId=22&categoryTypeId=1&collection=CHOGM&sortAttributeId=7&sortDescending=false#imageModal.
2. Ibid.

THE COMMONWEALTH AND THE EUROPEAN UNION IN THE 21ST CENTURY

3. Ibid.

4. See in particular chapter 10 of Mazower (2012, pp. 273–304). For an overview of recent historiographical discussions on the global role of international organisations, see, for instance, Iriye (2004) and Reinalda (2009); and thematic issues of international history journals (Kott, 2011; Rodogno et al., 2012).

5. Such studies include Hutchinson (2000), Barnett (2011) and Cox (2009); as well as other studies quoted in this article.

6. The dominant institutional focus, in its realist and functionalist versions, is discussed by Kott (2011). See also Fassin (2012).

7. Michael Barnett's attempt at such *longue-durée* analysis, although criticised for some of its shortcomings, is a useful example of this (Barnett, 2011). See also Rodogno (2012).

8. For an illustration of this contrast see Philippe Ryffman's and Michael Barnett's respective accounts (Ryfman, 2008; Barnett, 2011).

9. See also Barnett's chapter 'Saving slaves, sinners, savages, and societies' (Barnett, 2011, pp. 57–75).

10. Convention for the Amelioration of the Condition of the Wounded in Armies in the Field, 22 August 1864, https://www.icrc.org/ihl/INTRO/120?OpenDocument; see also Convention (I) for the Amelioration of the Condition of the Wounded and Sick in Armed Forces in the Field, 12 August 1949, https://www.icrc.org/applic/ihl/ihl.nsf/Article.xsp?action=openDocument&documentId=200E2B4090502A4AC12563CD00519EF8.

11. On this topic, see Finnemore's chapter (1999, pp. 149–168).

12. On the rise of nutritional sciences in international organisations, see Staples (2006, pp. 64–81).

13. See on this topic Johanna Siméant's thoughts on scholars' symbolic use of the end of the Cold War in Siméant and Dauvin (2004, p. 13).

14. For a contemporary account of the inclusion of disaster preparedness in humanitarian policy, see Fromuth (1988, p. 178).

15. See, for instance, the discussions in Weiss (2012).

16. For instance, for a study of the International Relief Union in a *longue-durée* framework, see Hutchinson (2000). On the creation of UNDRO, see Nishimoto (2014).

17. For a first-hand testimony on the history of UNDRO, see Peter Macalister-Smith (1980); see also Nishimoto (2014).

18. Resolution 66/232 of the United Nations Security Council (United Nations, 1966), 2006-152, Rhodesia, Miscellaneous Correspondence Part 2, COMSEC; *Report on the Work of the Sanctions Committee, January 1971–June 1973*, n.d., 2005-101 Ottawa Circular Papers, COMSEC, Arnold Smith Papers.

19. Minutes of Commonwealth Sanctions Committee Meeting, 10 December 1971, 2004-048 Rhodesia: Internal Affairs, COMSEC; ibid.; Report on the Meeting between Mr Anyaoku and Sir John Carter, Chairman of the Sanctions Committee, at the Guyana High Commission at 10.00 am, on 2 March 1972, n.d., 2004-48 Rhodesia, Internal Affairs, COMSEC; *Report on the Work of the Sanctions Committee, January 1971–June 1973*; Arnold Smith, Commonwealth Heads of Government Meeting, May/June 1975, Commonwealth Humanitarian Assistance to Southern Africa, Background Note by Secretary-General, n.d., 2006-141 Heads of Government Meeting 1975 Kingston Part 2, COMSEC, Arnold Smith Papers; Commonwealth Heads of Government Meeting, June 1977. Draft Report of the Sanctions Committee, July 1975–May 1977, n.d., 2009-161 Heads of Governments Meeting Lancaster House 1977, Part 2, COMSEC, Shridath Ramphal Papers.

20. Ottawa Final Communiqué, 1973, 2005-101 Ottawa Heads of Governments Meeting 1973, COMSEC.

21. *Report on the Work of the Sanctions Committee, January 1971–June 1973*; Ottawa Final Communiqué.

22. Commonwealth Assistance to Rhodesian Africans and Namibians: Rhodesia, n.d., 2007-140 Countries Aid to Mozambique, 1975–76, COMSEC, Shridath Ramphal Papers.

23. Commonwealth Secretariat (1987, p. 10); Commonwealth Assistance to Rhodesian Africans and Namibians, n.d., 2007-148, Southern Africa 1976, COMSEC, Shridath Ramphal Papers; Smith, Commonwealth Heads of Government Meeting, May/June 1975, Commonwealth Humanitarian Assistance to Southern Africa, Background Note by Secretary-General, p. 2.

24. Message from the High Commissioner of Zambia to A. Smith, 12 January 1973, 2006-152, Rhodesia, Miscellaneous Correspondence Part 1, COMSEC; Letter from A. Smith to High Commissioner of Zambia, 15 January 1973, 2006-152, Rhodesia, Miscellaneous Correspondence Part 1, COMSEC.

25. Emeka Anyaoku, Possible Relations with UN Sanctions Committee, 8 March 1972, 2004-066 Rhodesia Exchange with UN Sanctions Committee, COMSEC; Minutes of the Meeting of the Sanctions Committee,

THE COMMONWEALTH AND THE EUROPEAN UNION IN THE 21ST CENTURY

31 March 1976, 6, 2007-009 Sanctions Committee 1976 Circulated Papers and Minutes, Part 1, COM-SEC.

26. Arnold Smith, Telegram, 27 April 1974, 2006-141 Heads of Governments Meeting Kingston, Part 1, COMSEC, Arnold Smith Papers.

27. J. R. Syson, Letter to M. Malhoutra, 1 June 1977, 2008-013 HGM 1977 Background Papers, COMSEC; see also Commonwealth Assistance to Rhodesian Africans and Namibians; and Commonwealth Heads of Government Meeting, June 1977. Draft Report of the Sanctions Committee, July 1975–May 1977.

28. *Report on the Commonwealth Committee on Southern Africa, June 1977–June 1979*, n.d., 7–12, 2010-017 HGM 1979 Zambia Background Papers Part 2, COMSEC.

29. Aide Humanitaire Canadienne Aux Vietnamiens, *Présent 2e Édition Nationale*, 7 May 1970, Les Archives de Radio-Canada, http://archives.radio-canada.ca/guerres_conflits/guerre_vietnam/clips/6132/, accessed 14 April 2015.

30. Official assistance tripled between 1990 and 2000 (Barnett, 2011, p. 3).

31. On the recent history of the humanitarian sector, see Ryfman (2008).

32. On this topic, see the position of one of the founders of Médecins Sans Frontières (Brauman, 2009).

33. Treaty on the Functioning of the European Union (TFEU), Art. 214-2, in Cremona (2011, p. 13).

34. See Versluys (2009, p. 91).

35. See Darwin (1988, p. 235).

36. See Cox (2009).

37. The Harare Commonwealth Declaration (1991), http://assets.thecommonwealth.org/assetbank-common wealth/action/viewDownloadFile?CSRF=AC4sa3MAdMJk0IK5mrxS&returnUrl=viewSearchItem%3findex %3d1%261%3d1&id=19499, accessed 14 April 2015.

38. See also the denunciation of 'ethnic cleansing' and 'mass murder' in Bosnia-Herzegovina. The Auckland Communiqué (1995), http://assets.thecommonwealth.org/assetbank-commonwealth/action/viewAsset?id= 19554&index=6&total=36&view=viewSearchItem#imageModal, accessed 15 April 2015.

39. Ibid.

40. The Malta Communiqué (2005) Final Communiqué from the Commonwealth Heads of Government Meeting (CHOGM) in Malta, 25–27 November 2005.

41. Commonwealth Secretariat (2009).

42. Department for International Development (2011); Commonwealth Secretariat (2013).

43. The Durban Communiqué (1999), n.d., http://assets.thecommonwealth.org/assetbank-commonwealth/ac tion/viewAsset?id=19564&index=2&total=6&view=viewSearchItem; Kaberere (n.d.).

44. The Edinburgh Communiqué (1997), n.d., http://assets.thecommonwealth.org/assetbank-commonwealth/ac tion/viewAsset?id=19549&index=3&total=36&view=viewSearchItem#imageModal, accessed 15 April 2015.

45. Barnett (2011).

46. For a glimpse of such rebukes, see Short (2015); Commonwealth Secretariat (2013).

References

Adinolfi, C., Bassiouni, D., Lauritzsen, H. F. and Williams, H. R. (2005) Humanitarian response review, United Nations, August, reliefweb.int/sites/reliefweb.int/files/resources/Humanitarian%20Response%20Re view%20Commissioned%20by%20the%20UN%20Emergency%20Relief%20Coordinator%20and%20USG% 20for%20Humanitarian%20Affairs.pdf, accessed 17 April 2015.

Barnett, M. N. (2011) *Empire of Humanity: A History of Humanitarianism*. Ithaca, NY: Cornell University Press.

Barnett, M. N. and Weiss, T. G. (Eds) (2008) *Humanitarianism in Question: Politics, Power, Ethics*. Ithaca, NY: Cornell University Press.

Brauman, R. (2009) Emotion et action humanitaire, *Études*, 410(1), pp. 9–19.

Butler, L. J. (2002) *Britain and Empire: Adjusting to a Post-Imperial World*. London: I. B. Tauris.

Chabbott, C. (1999) Development INGOs, in J. Boli and G.M. Thomas (Eds.), *Constructing World Culture: International Nongovernmental Organizations since 1875*. Stanford: Stanford University Press, pp. 222–248.

Commonwealth Secretariat (1987) *The Commonwealth at the Summit: Communiqués of Commonwealth Heads of Government Meetings, 1944–1986*. London: Commonwealth Secretariat.

THE COMMONWEALTH AND THE EUROPEAN UNION IN THE 21ST CENTURY

Commonwealth Secretariat (2009) The Commonwealth Secretariat's Statement to the 2nd Global Platform on Disaster Risk Reduction, 16 June, http://www.preventionweb.net/files/globalplatform/ComsecStatement tothesecondsessionof.doc, accessed 17 April 2015.

Commonwealth Secretariat (2013) Commonwealth Secretariat Response to the DFID Multilateral Aid Review Update, 10 July, thecommonwealth.org/media/news/commonwealth-secretariat-response-dfid-multilateral-aid-review-update, accessed 17 April 2015.

Cox, R. (2009) Témoignage sur l'action humanitaire de l'Union européenne à travers l'expérience d'ECHO (European Community Humanitarian Office), *Matériaux pour l'histoire de Notre Temps*, 95(3), pp. 75–81.

Cremona, M. (2011) The EU and global emergencies: competence and instruments, in A. Antoniadis, R. Schütze and E. Spaventa (Eds), *The European Union and Global Emergencies: A Law and Policy Analysis*. Oxford: Bloomsbury, pp. 11–32.

Darwin, J. (1988) *Britain and Decolonisation: The Retreat from Empire in the Post-war World*. Basingstoke: Macmillan.

Dauvin, P. (2010) *La Communication des ONG Humanitaires*. Paris: L'Harmattan.

Department for International Development (2011) Multilateral aid review: assessment of the Commonwealth Secretariat, https://www.gov.uk/government/publications/multilateral-aid-review-commonwealth-secretariat-commsec, accessed 17 April 2015.

European Commission (1991) Commission decides to set up a European Office for Humanitarian Aid, 6 November, http://europa.eu/rapid/press-release_P-91-69_en.htm, accessed 8 July 2015.

Fassin, D. (2012) *Humanitarian Reason: A Moral History of the Present*. Berkeley: University of California Press.

Finnemore, M. (1999) Rules of war and wars of rules: the International Red Cross and the restraint of state violence, in J. Boli and G.M. Thomas (Eds.), *Constructing World Culture: International Nongovernmental Organizations since 1875*. Stanford: Stanford University Press, pp. 149–168.

Fromuth, P. J. (1988) *A Successor Vision: The United Nations of Tomorrow*. New York: University Press of America.

Haskell, T. L. (1985) Capitalism and the origins of the humanitarian sensibility, Part 1, *The American Historical Review*, 90(2), pp. 339–61.

Hutchinson, J.F. (2000) Disasters and the international order: earthquakes, humanitarians, and the Ciraolo Project, *The International History Review*, 22(1), pp. 1–36.

Iriye, A. (2004) *Global Community: The Role of International Organizations in the Making of the Contemporary World*. Berkeley: University of California Press.

Kaberere, J. (n.d.) *The Commonwealth Secretariat Support for Disaster Risk Reduction and Disaster Management in Member Countries*. London: Commonwealth Secretariat.

Kott, S. (2011) Les organisations internationales, terrains d'étude de la globalisation. Jalons pour une approche socio-historique, *Critique internationale*, 52(3), pp. 9–16.

Macalister-Smith, P. (1980) The future role of UNDRO? United Nations Economic and Social Council, July 1980, Statements and Annual Report of the UN Disaster Relief Co-Ordinator, *Disasters*, 4(4), pp. 377–379.

Mazower, M. (2012) *Governing the World: The History of an Idea*. London: Penguin Press.

McIntyre, D. (2001) Commonwealth legacy, in J.Brown and Wm R. Louis (Eds), *The Oxford History of the British Empire: Volume IV: The Twentieth Century*. Oxford: Oxford University Press, pp. 693–702.

Mendlesohn, F. J. (1999) The ethics of friends' relief work in republican Spain, *Quaker History*, 88(2), pp. 1–23.

Nishimoto, K. (2014) The role of international organizations in disaster response: a case study of recent earthquakes in Japan, in D. D. Caron, M. J. Kelly and A. Telesetsky (Eds.), *The International Law of Disaster Relief*. Cambridge: Cambridge University Press, pp. 295–313.

Orde, A. (1996) *The Eclipse of Great Britain. The United States and British Imperial Decline, 1895–1956*. Basingstoke: Palgrave.

Reinalda, B. (2009) *Routledge History of International Organizations: From 1815 to the Present Day*. London and New York: Routledge.

Rodogno, D. (2012) Empire of humanity: a history of humanitarianism by Michael Barnett, *Journal of International Organizations Studies*, 3(1), pp. 74–78.

Rodogno, D., Schulz, M., Vaïsse, M. (2012) Introduction: organisations internationales et ONG : coopération, rivalité, complémentarité de 1919 à nos jours—1, *Relations Internationales*, 151(3), pp. 3–9.

Roiron, V. (2013) Challenged Commonwealth? The decolonisation of Rhodesia, *Cercles*, 28, pp. 169–191.

Ryfman, P. (2008) *Une Histoire de L'humanitaire*. Paris: La Découverte.

Short, C. (2015) Reform of EU aid programme is overdue, *The Guardian*, 23 January.

Sicurelli, D. (2013) *The European Union's Africa Policies: Norms, Interests and Impact*. Farnham: Ashgate .

Siméant, J., and Dauvin, P. (2004) *O.N.G. et Humanitaire*. Paris: L'Harmattan.

Smith, A. (1981) *Stitches in Time: The Commonwealth in World Politics*. Don Mills, Canada: General Publishing.

Staples, A. L. S. (2006) *The Birth of Development: How the World Bank, Food And Agriculture Organization, And World Health Organization Have Changed the World 1945–1965*. Kent, OH: Kent State University Press.

Steets, J., Meier, C., Christensen, D., Kindergan, N. and Pfister, D. (2012) *Coordination to Save Lives: History and Emerging Challenges.*, United Nations Office for the Coordination of Humanitarian Affairs, docs.un ocha.org/sites/dms/Documents/Coordination%20to%20Save%20Lives%20History%20and%20Emerging% 20Challenges.pdf, accessed 15 April 2015.

Stewart, E. J. (2006) *The European Union and Conflict Prevention: Policy Evolution and Outcome* (Münster: LIT Verlag).

United Nations (1991) A/RES/46/182, 19 December, http://www.un.org/documents/ga/res/46/a46r182.htm, accessed 8 July 2015.

Versluys, H. (2009) European Union humanitarian aid, in J. Orbie (Ed.), *Europe's Global Role: External Policies of the European Union*. Farnham: Ashgate, pp. 91–116.

Weiss, T. G. (2012) *Humanitarian Intervention: Ideas in Action*. Cambridge: Polity Press.

The International Humanitarian Regime and its Discontents: India's Challenge

ANNE HAMMERSTAD
University of Kent, Canterbury, UK

ABSTRACT *In recent years, concerns over whether the humanitarian regime as we know it will survive a many-pronged challenge have spurred humanitarian organisations to embark on processes of soul-searching and innovation. With a steadily increasing aid budget and its more active and vocal role in development and humanitarian politics—and in global politics more generally—India has acquired the label of 'emerging' humanitarian actor. This article, however, shows that in many ways India has been a humanitarian pioneer, and connects the norms and values of the international humanitarian regime with India's own philosophical, religious and democratic traditions. It also discusses how Indian policy-makers have critiqued the current United Nations-led international humanitarian regime and investigates how the government of an increasingly powerful and influential Commonwealth country from the South interacts with an international regime created in Europe. For many Indian policy-makers, current humanitarian practices are tainted by what they see as North American and European interventionist and highly political agendas in the South. The article concludes that while there is still a lot to be said for a global, multilateral humanitarian regime led by the United Nations, it need not be Western-biased, either in theory or in practice.*

Introduction: Challenges to Humanitarianism

In recent years, there has been an intense debate on the future of humanitarian action. Attacks on the legitimacy of the international humanitarian regime have come from many and disparate corners. They range from proponents of the US wars in Afghanistan and Iraq to vehement critics of the same; from post-colonial intellectuals in the South to liberal interventionists in the North. This debate goes on in the context of ever more extreme attacks on the idea of humanitarianism, such as the targeted killing of humanitarian workers in war zones. Concerns over whether the humanitarian regime as we know it will survive this many-pronged challenge have spurred humanitarian organisations themselves to embark on processes of soul-searching and innovation, recently through the United Nation's (UN's) World Humanitarian Summit, a global programme of regional consultations, online interactions and expert reports building up to a summit meeting in Istanbul in 2016.

Among the challengers to the international humanitarian regime is a set of 'emerging' state actors from the global South. During the past decade, countries such as India,

Brazil, China and several Gulf States have become significant donors in the fields of international development and humanitarian aid. In 1991–92, before India embarked on two decades of substantial economic growth, India's overseas aid budget stood at INR 1 billion (Quadir, 2013, p. 322). This increased to INR 34.71 billion in 2011–12 and INR 94.34 billion in 2014–15 (Indian Development Cooperation Research, IDCR, 2015b, p. 1). These figures cover development and emergency assistance, including loans and grants, provided by India to other countries, disbursed through its Ministry of External Affairs (MEA). The overall aid figure is higher, because the MEA figures do not cover assistance to refugees on India's own soil, or aid provided by India's federal states, e.g. aid from Tamil Nadu to the Tamil areas of Sri Lanka.

Because of the explosive growth in its aid budget, and owing to its more active and vocal role in development and humanitarian politics—and in global politics more generally—India has acquired the label of 'emerging' humanitarian actor. As we shall see, India has a long history of humanitarian efforts, so this label is only correct inasmuch as it denotes India's higher public profile in international humanitarian forums. India's 'emergence' has taken place just as humanitarian politics has become more contested than ever. Many Indian policy-makers and analysts suggest this is not a coincidence. They argue that the arrival of India and other states in the South as important humanitarian actors and donors constitutes a fundamental challenge to the workings of the current UN-led international humanitarian regime. This regime is skewed, they argue, towards the values and interests of the 20 or so traditional donors who provide the vast majority of the funds bankrolling the main UN and non-governmental humanitarian organisations and their work. For instance, the UN High Commissioner for Refugees (UNHCR), which is one of the world's largest humanitarian actors, has since its inception been mainly funded by the same group of North American and Western European states. The three top donors to UNHCR's 2013 budget were the US (36%), Japan (9%) and the European Union (7%), with Kuwait the only non-Western country (apart from Japan) making it to the list of donors that contribute more than 1% of the US$3 billion received by the refugee agency that year (UNHCR, 2014, p. 109).

This article investigates how the government of an increasingly powerful and influential Commonwealth country from the South interacts with an international regime created in Europe. Somewhat simplified, the premise of the critique by sceptical Indian policy-makers, as well as many Indian analysts, is that the humanitarian regime, despite its universal credentials, is yet another sphere of international politics in which rich, established powers of the global North act on the South—another aspect of an expansionist and ultimately self-serving agenda (see, e.g. Chanana, 2009). This is not a new claim. In 1997, Alex de Waal (1997) coined the term 'the disaster relief industry', and in 2012 Teju Cole (2012) satirised the 'White-saviour industrial complex'. But it is an important critique. India has a potentially powerful voice in shaping the future of the international humanitarian regime. It is a stable and democratic southern power with a growing aid budget and a long history of development cooperation and emergency assistance (despite its 'emerging' label). It is therefore valuable to examine how India perceives, and interacts with, the international humanitarian regime. Its public position as a newly influential humanitarian actor is to make it clear that it is not prepared to fit meekly into pre-established rules and norms, set by traditional donors in the European Union (EU) and North America, through the UN.

THE COMMONWEALTH AND THE EUROPEAN UNION IN THE 21ST CENTURY

I begin by setting out the institutions and norms that underpin the international humanitarian regime as we know it today. This regime was forged in 19th century Europe, beginning with the work of Henri Dunant and the establishment of the Red Cross movement, but has evolved considerably since then, towards a more interventionist and rights-based normative framework.

The next part looks at India as a humanitarian actor, historically and now. It asks how India's approach differs from the international regime as it emerged, first, from the historical experiences of war and humanitarian disaster in Europe, and, then, as the experiences and practices forged in Europe spread across the globe after World War II. This discussion makes it clear that the differences are not always as clear as the rhetoric suggests, and that in many ways India has been a humanitarian pioneer, from its 'humanitarian intervention' in East Pakistan in 1971 to its emphasis on development partnerships, capacity building and technical assistance already in the 1960s.

In fact, India subscribes with very few exceptions to the norms and values of the international humanitarian regime, since these coincide with India's own philosophical, religious and democratic traditions. But it deems many current humanitarian practices as tainted by what it sees as North American and European interventionist, and highly political agendas in the South. India's critique is symptomatic of many southern states' lack of trust in the motivations of the large international humanitarian organisations, after two decades of a particularly interventionist foreign policy by the handful of donors, notably the US and the EU, that fund the vast majority of global humanitarian operations.

The International Humanitarian Regime

Humanitarian assistance is aid provided to victims of sudden-onset natural or human-made disasters such as floods, famines or war. It is often called emergency aid, to highlight its short-term, quick-impact goals of saving lives and alleviating suffering, in contrast to the longer-term goals of development aid. The term 'complex emergency' emphasises the particular difficulties of responding to humanitarian disasters that unfold in the midst of war or other forms of large-scale political violence, where a humanitarian response takes place alongside political, and sometimes military, efforts by outside actors to stop the violence.

It is in this latter scenario that humanitarian action has come in for the harshest criticism, and it is for this reason that much of the discussion in this article will focus on humanitarian aid during complex emergencies. In a highly critical article on the role of humanitarian agencies in the Iraq war, Anderson (2004, p. 41) noted that combatants no longer heed the sanctity of the 'noble concept of inviolability' of humanitarian action. Inviolability (and hence the safety of humanitarian workers) rests on two pillars: 'neutrality, which is the assurance given by humanitarian agencies that their efforts are not in military support of either side, and impartiality, which means such effort is rendered to the noncombatant population of each side without distinction and according to need' (Anderson, 2004, p. 41). These pillars, Anderson (2004, p. 42) argued, have been undermined by an 'intellectual and moral crisis: there is growing conceptual confusion over what inviolability is and what morally justifies it'.

THE COMMONWEALTH AND THE EUROPEAN UNION IN THE 21ST CENTURY

This theme, of how humanitarian impartiality, neutrality and inviolability during war have become undermined, pre-dates the post-9/11 period of the 'War on Terror'. It caused much debate in the first decade after the end of the Cold War, and was discussed—although with less vehemence—in the 1980s (Hammerstad, 2014). But was there ever a golden age when humanitarian inviolability existed, and when there was universal agreement on the norms and institutions on which this inviolability rests?

The international humanitarian regime as we know it today was created in 19th century Europe, when Henri Dunant founded the Red Cross movement and work began on what was to become the Geneva Conventions. Known as the Laws of War, and later as International Humanitarian Law, they set out rules for how to treat civilians, the wounded, prisoners of war and other non-combatants. The rules also covered humanitarian workers, who were given humanitarian inviolability as long as their work was solely in aid of non-combatants, something the many parties to the endless European conflicts could—at least in theory—agree was to the common good.

From this European past, the Laws of War gradually attained global reach. In the aftermath of World War II, most of the world's states signed the Geneva Conventions. The UN, another post-war addition to international society, soon spawned agencies with humanitarian assistance as part of their mandates, such as the UNHCR, the UN Children's Fund (UNICEF) and the World Food Programme (WFP). Some have suggested that the following few post-war decades were a golden age where the moral legitimacy of humanitarian workers was generally accepted across the world. As one example, in 1970 both the Biafran separatists and government forces allowed smallpox vaccination campaigns to take place in the midst of Nigeria's otherwise terribly brutal civil war. This stands in stark contrast to today's targeting and killing of polio vaccination workers by the Pakistani Taliban and Northern Nigeria's Boko Haram.

This example apart, criticism of the international humanitarian regime has existed from its inception, and attacks have always come from several sides. On the one hand, Realists from Clausewitz onwards have argued that the stakes of warfare are so high for combatants that there are times when they cannot let themselves be constrained by considerations of the well-being of civilians, or adhere to the niceties of humanitarian neutrality. This form of reasoning led the US government to camouflage its search for Osama Bin Laden in Pakistan in the guise of a polio vaccination campaign.

Some critics argue that neutrality and impartiality are a chimera, because from a practical point of view aid to civilians also benefits combatants—at best by allowing warring parties to concentrate on the war effort while others take care of civilian misery, at worst by letting combatants channel humanitarian resources to their military effort. Others argue that combatants and non-combatants are not always distinguishable, or that it is not always desirable to make the distinction, as the Allied forces decided when they fire-bombed German cities in an attempt to weaken German support for the Nazi regime's war effort.

On the other side of the spectrum are those who argue against humanitarian impartiality and neutrality from the point of view of universal ethics. By negotiating access and protection from all sides in a conflict, and by not taking sides, humanitarian organisations can give recognition and stature to illegitimate and brutal regimes or rebels, ranging from Nazi Germany to Bosnian Serb paramilitary groups and Sierra Leonean rebels. This argument strengthened after the end of the Cold War, when humanitarian action and military intervention took place simultaneously to reduce human suffering *and* remove the regimes or rebel groups causing the suffering in Haiti, Somalia, the former Yugoslavia, Sierra Leone, Liberia and Libya, to mention but a few.

Humanitarian organisations operating in the midst of war have always performed a tightrope act between those asking them to take a moral stance (e.g. for democracy, human rights, the 'right side' in a war) and those accusing them of politicising aid and of aiding and abetting the other, enemy, side in a conflict. While this has always been a challenge, this challenge has now reached the stage of a crisis of legitimacy, due to a combination of factors. First is the emergence of a more fragmented international politics, with several power centres, after the end of the Cold War. Second is the more frequent, large-scale and intrusive nature of humanitarian operations in the post-Cold War period, conducted by large international organisations with multi-billion-dollar budgets. The third important factor is the reduced legitimacy of Western interventionism after the US-led wars in Afghanistan and Iraq after 9/11, which also tainted humanitarian organisations as complicit in this interventionist enterprise.

India as a Humanitarian Actor

For most of its history as an independent state, India has been better known as a receiver, not provider, of aid. In monetary terms (if not per capita), India has been termed 'the largest recipient in history', with around US$55 billion in foreign aid flowing into the country between 1951 and 1992 (*Economist*, 2011). It is a less known fact that India also has a long history as an aid provider and donor. In 1971, it hosted around 10 million destitute refugees fleeing a genocidal campaign in East Pakistan, while receiving dismally inadequate support from the rest of the world. In November 1971, India invaded East Pakistan to end the genocide on (particularly Hindu) Bengalis by the Pakistani military and to ensure East Pakistan's secession and the creation of independent Bangladesh. With its mix of humanitarian and power political motivations, this was one of the earliest 'humanitarian interventions' of the post-war period, making India something of a humanitarian pioneer.

India has also received, and still hosts, substantial numbers of refugees from Tibet (including the Dalai Lama), Myanmar, Sri Lanka and Afghanistan, and has done so with little assistance from the UN refugee agency, UNHCR, or other international actors. India is not a signatory to the UN Refugee Convention. Nevertheless, it has a relatively good record on its treatment of refugees from neighbouring countries. Outside its own region, India has long been a top provider of UN peacekeepers to operations all over the world. It was the third largest troop-contributing country in 2014, providing 7,923 uniformed personnel to UN peacekeeping operations (United Nations Development and Planning Organisation, 2014). It has a long-standing Technical and Economic Training programme (ITEC), established in 1964 as a way to share Indian development knowledge and technical expertise with other poor countries through training and partnerships on a modest budget (IDCR, 2015a). Thus, India is also a pioneer of the partnership and capacity-building model currently favoured by the international aid community.

After its economic reforms of the early 1990s set off a long burst of economic growth, India became not only an important aid actor, but also a significant aid donor. By 2014–15, its earlier aid flagship programme, ITEC, constituted less than 3% of India's aid budget (IDCR, 2015a). From 2001 onwards, India has been one of the top

THE COMMONWEALTH AND THE EUROPEAN UNION IN THE 21ST CENTURY

five donors to Afghanistan (Chanana, 2009, p. 11). It runs one of the most successful post-conflict humanitarian projects in northern Sri Lanka, building housing for displaced Tamils. It has also rebuilt the railway line to Jaffna in the far north of that country. It is a major donor to other neighbours, Bhutan and Nepal, and it has dramatically increased its aid to sub-Saharan African countries over the past decade.

A considerable body of research exists on India as a development aid donor (see, e.g. the work of Delhi-based research programmes such as IDCR, and Forum for Indian Development Cooperation). Until recently, its role as a humanitarian actor had received less attention, an early exception being Price (2005). While India's humanitarian efforts are less significant in monetary terms than its development aid, its increasingly active role as a humanitarian donor and its status as a long-established southern democracy mean that India's position and views on the future of the international humanitarian regime are significant.

India's Humanitarian Rhetoric

India likes to characterise itself as a partner, not a donor. Indeed, Indian officials often prefer to talk about 'South–South development cooperation' in a spirit of solidarity and mutual benefit, rather than Indian assistance, even if the aid provided is only flowing in one direction, from India to its beneficiary. After being at the receiving end of development aid for decades, it decided in the early 21st century largely to reject the Western aid model for its own development.

A watershed in India's transition from recipient to donor came when it refused international humanitarian assistance in the days immediately after the December 2004 Indian Ocean tsunami, while quickly offering its own assistance to Sri Lanka, the Maldives and other affected neighbours (Price, 2005, p. 16). Later on, India solicited funds for rehabilitation and reconstruction work from a few large donor bodies, particularly the Asian Development Bank (which provided US$200 million) and the World Bank (which granted India US$528.5 million). The Delhi government also approached the European Commission in early 2005. The Commission's humanitarian agency, ECHO, responded positively. It included India in its January 2005 allocation of €80 million to tsunami-hit countries and commended Indian authorities for having 're-sponded to the emergency phase in a robust and timely manner' (ECHO, 2005, p. 7). In all, ECHO contributed €12 million to India's recovery efforts (compared with €42.5 million to Sri Lanka and €60 million to Indonesia).[1]

Successive Indian governments have endeavoured to set India's own approach apart from what it considers to be the paternalistic, high-handed and culturally insensitive aid practices of international aid agencies. India's rhetoric of equal partnerships, rather than the hierarchical donor–recipient relationship, is accompanied by an emphasis on the pre-eminence of national sovereignty. India likes to characterise its aid model as demand-driven—and, in its view, the only legitimate demander is the sitting government of the disaster-stricken country, not civil society organisations or UN agencies. This means that India usually provides aid directly to governments, not via national or international non-governmental organisations (NGOs), although it channels an increasing proportion of its humanitarian aid through the UN, when this is what the recipient country prefers (IDCR, 2015b, p. 4).

THE COMMONWEALTH AND THE EUROPEAN UNION IN THE 21ST CENTURY

India's official discourse on the values and principles of humanitarian aid are not that different from those of the UN or traditional donors. All of India's religions, not least Hinduism, espouse norms that underpin humanitarianism, including the value of selfless acts, charity, compassion and hospitality to strangers without regard to one's own interest. The *Mahabharata*—a Sanskrit epic poem, philosophical dialogue and sacred text—concludes that *anrishamsya* (compassion) is the highest *dharma* (duty, virtue, or doing the right thing) (Das, 2009, p. 269). The *Mahabharata* also includes searching discussions, most notably between Krishna and Arjuna, on the Laws of War: on when it is morally right to fight, and what the moral limits are to how one can fight, once war has started. From the point of view of ancient Indian moral philosophy, then, there is nothing particularly Western about humanitarian norms.

Indian officials, both during the 10-year tenure of the previous Prime Minister, Manmohan Singh, and under the current leadership of Prime Minister Narendra Modi, have been eager to underline the combination of uniqueness and universality of Indian cultural values and foreign policy outlook. India's values are unique in that they are rooted in Sanskrit philosophy and tradition, but they are universal due to the cosmopolitan (rather than communitarian) nature of this philosophy. During the aftermath of the Indian Ocean tsunami in December 2004, the MEA released a report on India's considerable regional relief efforts. The introduction to the report set out the normative foundation for India's aid efforts, emphasising both neighbourly and global ties that bind:

South and Southeast Asia are a region joined by history and by deep-rooted social and cultural ties. Centuries of interaction have created a natural sense of affinity and empathy among the people of the region. It is, therefore, only natural that they come together in the face of this unprecedented disaster. This vividly demonstrates the truth of the ancient Sanskrit saying 'Vasudhaiva Kutumbakam', or that the world is one family (MEA, 2005a).

This motif of *Vasudhaiva Kutumbakam* was also pursued by Prime Minister Narendra Modi in his maiden speech to the UN General Assembly in September 2014: 'Every nation's world view is shaped by its civilization and philosophical tradition. India's ancient wisdom sees the world as one family'. Linking this to India's humanitarian and development aid, he continued a little later on: 'India is part of the developing world, but we are prepared to share our modest resources with those countries that need this assistance as much as we do' (Modi, 2014).

There is no doubt that India's government—as well as its voters—perceive humanitarian aid as a moral duty, and hence as a legitimate and desirable aspect of India's relations with other states, particularly in its own region. But India's foreign policy-makers are also open about linking this moral duty with pragmatic foreign policy interests, much in the way that 'middle powers' such as Norway and Sweden understand their large aid budgets and support of multilateral institutions as intrinsic to their soft power (Hammerstad, 2012). Humanitarian assistance is about demonstrating India's capabilities and expertise, as India proudly did when it dispensed, through its navy, considerable aid to neighbouring countries after the Indian Ocean tsunami (see, e.g. MEA, 2005b). It is about mutual benefit, strengthening political and economic ties with friendly nations, and—when possible, such as after the 2010 floods in Pakistan—reaching out to less friendly nations in the hope of improving relations. It is about bolstering its presence and influence in international bodies, as when it highlights its contribution of more than 180,000 soldiers to 49 different UN peacekeeping missions over the decades to argue (not unreasonably) for a seat on the UN Security Council (*Economic Times*, 2015). Last but not least, it is part of India's sense of 'emerging power' rivalry with China, both in their shared neighbourhood and globally.

As is the case with other humanitarian donor states, a mix of compassionate and pragmatic motivations lies behind India's humanitarian decision-making. That said, there are other aspects of India's rhetoric on humanitarian action that set it apart from the discourse of European and North American donor governments. Most noticeably, India promotes a strict interpretation of non-intervention in the sovereign affairs of other states. Humanitarian assistance should be offered only to governments that ask for it. Owing to its commitment to national sovereignty, India advocates a humanitarian duty, but only as a duty to *respond* to requests for help by the governments of disaster-stricken states, not to use humanitarian arguments to trump state sovereignty. This non-judgemental approach was on show in 2008, when India was one of only a few foreign states (including China) allowed by Myanmar's military junta to provide assistance to the victims of Cyclone Nargis (Meier and Murthy, 2011, p. 19).

During the 2005 World Summit on the 'Responsibility to Protect' (R2P), India expressed strong reservations against the idea of a 'humanitarian imperative'. As Hall has stated:

> India's then Ambassador to the UN, Nirupam Sen, launched an 'eleventh hour assault' on the concept [of R2P] at the summit, attacking its legal foundations and even the name itself, which Sen called 'patronizing and offensive'. Although India did not move to block the final agreement, the attack reflected ongoing worries about the ultimate object of R2P and whether it would prove open to abuse by the powerful. (Hall, 2013, p. 93)

The debate on R2P during the 2005 World Summit was part of a larger theme of UN reform, including reform of the Security Council. India has demanded a permanent seat on the Security Council since 1955 (the first and only time the Security Council was expanded was in 1963, with four additional non-permanent members). Its diplomatic endeavours to achieve this have been hampered by a dearth of strong allies in its own region, the suspicion of China and hostility of Pakistan to its ambition, and the lack of sustained diplomatic pressure maintained by its own foreign policy establishment. Since the 2014 election, the new government under Prime Minister Narendra Modi has pursued a Security Council seat with renewed vigour, using India's more prominent humanitarian role, and particularly its participation in UN peacekeeping operations, as a key argument:

> By any objective criteria such as population, territorial size, GDP, economic potential, civilizational legacy, cultural diversity, political system and past and on-going contributions to the activities of the UN—especially to UN peacekeeping operations—India is eminently suited for permanent membership of an expanded UNSC. (MEA, n.d. [2014/15])

The Indian government has also stepped up its bilateral efforts to garner support for a Security Council seat. India has good relations with the EU, including the two

European permanent Security Council members. India has deep and long-established—if complicated—ties to the UK and strong trade and business links to both the UK and France (including signing a large arms deal with the latter in April 2015). The EU remains an important market for Indian goods. But in terms of global politics and long-term foreign policy strategy, Europe tends to be seen as a wilting, or at least stagnant force. India sees its relationship with the US as strategically much more important, not least because of the two countries' mutual concern with China's role in its neighbourhood and its territorial claims against most of its neighbours, including India.

Despite India's continued public criticism of great power interventionism, and a history of mutual distrust,[2] India and the US have grown closer together since the end of the Cold War. Their relationship has strengthened on every level over the past decade, and particularly over the past year, with Prime Minister Modi keen to forge a personal relationship with President Barak Obama. Despite India's reluctance to support many of the US administration's foreign policy decisions, such as using aerial bombardment against ISIS in Iraq and Syria, Obama has publicly supported India's quest for a permanent seat on the Security Council. India, on its side, has been careful not to be obstructionist in its anti-interventionist agenda. The US and the EU have appreciated the mostly pragmatic and cautious manner in which India has steered through the highly polarised diplomatic environment caused by the conflicts in places such as Iraq, Libya, Syria and Ukraine.

Another outcome of India's strong commitment to national sovereignty is its reluctance to describe its assistance to victims of war as *humanitarian* assistance, instead using terms such as disaster relief or even development cooperation. Meier and Murthy (2011, p. 6) suggest that 'India's "disaster relief" rhetoric is possibly deliberate in order to avoid international political controversies associated with giving aid during civil war situations'.

India's dedication to non-interference in the sovereign affairs of states and its view that the delivery of humanitarian aid should be strictly non-political with no strings attached (such as demands for regime change or democratisation) hark back to an earlier time. Western donors, international NGOs and UN agencies have become stronger in their demands to deal with 'root causes' of humanitarian disasters such as refugee crises, and more frequently advocate military humanitarian intervention if governments do not allow outside access to victim populations (Hammerstad, 2014). Meanwhile, India and other emerging humanitarian actors have resisted this development of mixing human rights and humanitarianism.

India's Humanitarian Practices

How does India's humanitarian rhetoric fit India's behaviour as a humanitarian donor and actor? I begin by discussing the role of self-interest, conditionalities and interventionism in India's decisions to provide humanitarian aid, before looking at India's complicated relationship with the UN, the Commonwealth and other multilateral organisations.

Most of India's aid budget remains development assistance, and most of that is bilateral, state-to-state aid free of political conditionalities, but usually linked to Indian business or investment interests. Until the creation of the Development Partnership Administration (DPA) within the MEA in 2012, there was no central handling of India's aid budget. Funding decisions were mostly ad hoc and left to the powerful heads of the MEA's regional and country desks.

On the creation of the DPA, former Foreign Secretary Lalit Mansingh commented that '[t]he fact that the DPA division is located in the ministry of external affairs shows it is in sync with our foreign policy objectives of transforming India into a global player'. Mansingh suggested that India increasingly targeted its aid to bolster its economic and strategic interests (quoted in Roche, 2012). This view is echoed by Price (2005, p. 18), with a stronger tinge of realpolitik: 'It is clear that India perceives its assistance strategy largely in terms of self-interest, primarily since that is how it perceives other donors to have treated India'. Chanana (2009, p. 11) describes India's 'new consciousness of aid as an instrument of foreign policy. Through aid, India hopes to build new alliances and further its trade, energy and political interests. It also hopes to present the country as powerful and self-reliant'.

Looking at where India's development aid goes, a strong element of self-interest is clear. India's biggest aid programmes are in the energy sector, reflecting the energy needs of its fast-growing economy and population. Furthermore, Indian aid goes mostly to neighbours, and particularly to neighbours over which India wields, or hopes to wield (in the case of Afghanistan and Myanmar), considerable influence. 'Nearly 83 percent of the total grants and loans (or INR 78 billion) India extended in 2014–15 globally were to the following five nations: Afghanistan (INR 6.76 billion), Bhutan (INR 60 billion), Sri Lanka (INR 5 billion), Myanmar (INR 3.3 billion) and Nepal (INR 4.5 billion)' (IDCR, 2015b, p. 2).

Such self-interest is not the same as conditionalities, however. India is careful to promote its aid projects as mutually beneficial—in everybody's, not just its own, self-interest. It shows in practice, as well as theory, a willingness to be reactive to recipient requests, such as when it agreed to construct Afghanistan's new parliament building.

India's humanitarian assistance differs from its development aid. The figures are a lot smaller, and India continues to be a net recipient, not donor, of humanitarian aid. Perhaps surprisingly, given the intellectual critique of the UN offered by many Indian officials, India channels much of its humanitarian aid through the UN and other multilateral organisations.[3] The country's own economic interests are less on show in its humanitarian decisions than in its development assistance, although India provides aid in kind when it can, for instance preferring to provide batches of medicines produced by its own pharmaceutical industry rather than monetary donations.

Self-interest also guides where India targets its humanitarian aid. Its donation to the relief effort after the 2005 devastations of Hurricane Katrina in the US was both a show of solidarity and a symbol of India's political and economic rise. India has contributed to the international aid effort after natural disasters across the world, usually through the UN. It often avoids major involvement in complex emergencies, because of the political controversies such emergencies usually cause. This global reach combined with prudence bolster its reputation as a good global citizen without aligning it too closely with perceived Western interventionist agendas. As such, it contributes to India's ambitions to become a global power and southern champion.

But the vast majority of India's humanitarian aid efforts take place within its own neighbourhood, most notably in Afghanistan and Sri Lanka.[4] Perhaps the best way to understand India's humanitarian assistance to its neighbours is as clout with a friendly face. It contributes to friendly inter-state relations in a troubled region, and improves

India's relations with neighbours to the East after decades of relative isolation from Southeast Asia. It presents India as a responsible and non-aggressive neighbour, thus increases its soft power and legitimacy as a regional great power. In sensitive situations, such as post-war reconstruction in Afghanistan and flood relief in Pakistan, it always offers aid with a strong show of respect for national sovereignty. This has included channelling the aid through the UN or other multilateral organisations when the recipient government asks for it.

The last point highlights how the suspicion towards the UN's humanitarian agencies, often displayed in Indian official rhetoric, is less visible in practice. A recent report notes a steep rise in India's contributions to multilateral organisations. 'The Government of India's contributions to international organizations such as the United Nations, SAARC and the Commonwealth Foundation among others have increased from INR 1.82 billion in FY [fiscal year] 2010–11 to INR 4 billion in FY 2014–15, representing an increase of 140 percent over a four year period' (IDCR, 2015b, p. 4).

There is a clear distinction between how India interacts with international humanitarian organisations abroad and on its own territory. At the same time as India regularly works through the UN in its humanitarian efforts in other countries, it keeps UN actors —as well as other international humanitarian organisations such as the International Committee of the Red Cross (ICRC) and Médecins Sans Frontières (MSF)—on its own soil on a tight leash. India is a politically difficult country in which to operate for these organisations. The UN refugee agency, UNHCR, for instance, has an office in Delhi, but is not allowed to operate in refugee-hosting border areas, such as Mizoram, which hosts a large number of Chin refugees from Myanmar. India has not signed up to the UN Refugee Convention. It nevertheless prides itself on conforming to the Convention's fundamental principle of *non-refoulement*. UNHCR officials tend on the whole to agree with this, and view India as a potentially important southern ally in its task to improve standards of refugee protection across the world. Its attempts to create partnerships with the Indian government have so far yielded little response.

India's relationship to the Commonwealth organisation is symptomatic of its general approach to international organisations. In 1949, it remained as the Commonwealth's first republican member, refusing to pledge allegiance to the British Crown. With this, it ensured the organisation's transformation (and hence survival) from the British Commonwealth, a symbol of imperial reach, to a relatively egalitarian and somewhat eclectic collection of states brought together by historical and linguistic ties. It is easy to imagine a trajectory in which India would have become the leading member of the Commonwealth. Indeed, it looked as if this might happen when Kamalesh Sharma, an Indian diplomat, took over the helm as Secretary-General in 2008 (re-elected for a second and last term in 2012). In the run-up to his election, India increased its financial contributions to the Commonwealth and won the bid to host the 2010 Commonwealth Games in New Delhi (Kreling, 2009). Since then, however, interest has dropped again, although it is too early to say whether the more vigorous foreign policy of the Modi government will also benefit the Commonwealth organisation.

The Indian government's attitude to the Commonwealth springs from its state-centric and sovereignty-conscious foreign policy outlook. When observers have called for India to provide leadership to a frail Commonwealth organisation (e.g. *Economist*, 2013), they have not taken into account India's reluctance to support strong and activist international organisations. India's defence of national sovereignty and non-interference,

THE COMMONWEALTH AND THE EUROPEAN UNION IN THE 21ST CENTURY

and its suspicion of neo-colonial agendas, are displayed in the MEA's briefing note on the Commonwealth (MEA, 2013). The note shows that when India brings its voice to bear in Commonwealth forums, it is more often than not to ensure that the organisation retains a more modest, non-political and non-confrontational mode of operation. The MEA note describes India's efforts to circumscribe the role of civil society organisations at Commonwealth Heads of Government Meetings, noting the 'hidden agendas of some of the NGOs, dubious sources of their funding, as well as lack of accountability in the functioning of many NGOs and un-representativeness of their voice as compared to the governments' (MEA, 2013, p. 8). The note also makes clear that although India supports efforts to promote good governance, human rights and conflict resolution, it does not view the Commonwealth organisation as necessarily the most suitable body for such pursuits. It endorses quiet diplomacy and consensus building, and only cautiously supports suspension from the Commonwealth in extreme situations, particularly after political coups d'état. Returning to its preference for the non-political, it suggests that development, rather than 'political goals', should be the Commonwealth's main focus:

> The diversion of the Commonwealth's budget from developmental to political goals has also brought out the divide between the developing and developed countries, raising questions whether the Commonwealth is losing relevance for a majority of its members. (MEA, 2013, p. 5)

Considering the Commonwealth's modest budget (India was the organisation's fourth largest donor in 2013, contributing just under US$4 million), such a focus on development goals would have the perhaps unintended consequence of retaining the Commonwealth organisation's relatively low international profile.

Conclusion: A Decentralised Humanitarian System

This article has shown that the differences between India and traditional humanitarian donors in Europe and North America are in many ways smaller than Indian rhetoric suggests and international humanitarian organisations fear. India pursues the same mix of foreign policy interests and humanitarian instincts as traditional donors do, with some variation. On the one hand, in diplomatic forums, India objects strongly to Western interventionism and fears humanitarian arguments can cover for neo-imperialist ambitions. This is reflected in the strict conditions under which international humanitarian organisations such as the UNHCR, ICRC and MSF are allowed to operate within India's own borders.

Overall, India's own aid policy (which continues to be mostly development aid) stands apart somewhat from Western donors, and India has not joined the Organisation for Economic Cooperation and Development (OECD) Development Assistance Committee (DAC). Indian aid tends to be demand-driven, bilateral, unconditional and grounded in an ethos of South–South solidarity—although it is clearly also meant to create business and trade opportunities for India in the recipient country, and more so in the past couple of decades. That said, in its own neighbourhood, strategic reasoning has always accompanied humanitarian motivations.

THE COMMONWEALTH AND THE EUROPEAN UNION IN THE 21ST CENTURY

Despite the sometimes hostile rhetoric, India's behaviour as a humanitarian actor does not undermine the international humanitarian regime. India often channels its humanitarian efforts through the UN and other multilateral organisations. Furthermore, despite its anti-interventionist stance, India has been something of a pioneer of humanitarian intervention itself, when complex emergencies in its own neighbourhood have aroused a sense of empathy with ethnic cousins, coupled with a perception of threats to its vital interests. This was the case in 1971, when India invaded East Pakistan in aid of the East Bengali population. India's airlift in 1987 of humanitarian aid to civilian Tamils in Jaffna during the Sri Lankan civil war could also be described as a humanitarian intervention (Meier and Murthy, 2011, p. 4). Such actions are the exception, not the rule, of India's humanitarian practices. But, in a similar manner to US and EU decisions to intervene in places such as the former Yugoslavia, Haiti and Afghanistan, such exceptionalism tends to rise to the fore when India's vital security interests are perceived to be at stake.

What then is India challenging, when it critiques the international humanitarian regime? I suggest two issues are at stake. The first is India's lack of trust in Western agendas in the South. The second is India's own global ambitions as an emerging power. The sense that the UN is dominated by the US and its allies, with goals aligned to Western interests and an overly interventionist agenda, is real-felt, even if it sometimes is used as a rhetorical tool. India is not antagonistic to the US or the EU on the whole. India has long campaigned for a permanent seat on the UN Security Council, and after five decades as an intellectual leader of the non-aligned movement during the Cold War, it has aligned its foreign policy more clearly over the past two decades with Europe and, particularly, the US.

But India will only sign up to international regimes if it perceives it can interact within these regimes on an equal basis to established powers. While existing DAC members would like to see India included in their club of like-minded donors (see, e.g. OECD, 2014, p. 9), India suspects that it would have little say within the walls of this club, since its rules will already have been established according to the preferences of pre-existing members. Instead, India may contribute to the trend towards a decentralised, rather than unitary, humanitarian system, with 'regional humanitarian powers' playing an increasingly important role in their own neighbourhoods. This does not mean India will be an obstructionist presence in the field of international development or humanitarian cooperation, but that it prefers looser ties, such as being a 'key partner' of the OECD (together with Brazil, China, Indonesia and South Africa), rather than a DAC member.

As long as regional humanitarian powers subscribe to the fundamental principles of humanitarian action—needs-based action that respects the dignity of victims of natural or human-made disasters—a decentralised humanitarian regime need not be a negative development. It would allow countries such as India to foster a strong, home-grown rather than imported version of universal values, drawn from its own cultural and philosophical traditions. This would improve the legitimacy of the international humanitarian regime, and it would help to overcome resentment against cultural imperialism often directed at humanitarian organisations.

There is a risk, however, that a regionalised humanitarian regime will also become a more selective—and, in fact, more politically motivated—regime. India has a better track record than China or the Gulf States in adhering to universal humanitarian

THE COMMONWEALTH AND THE EUROPEAN UNION IN THE 21ST CENTURY

principles and standards for good humanitarian practice. But there are clear dangers involved in a regionalised international humanitarian regime, where the provision of aid to victims of humanitarian disasters depends on the motivations and interests of great regional powers in their own backyards. This is particularly the case for man-made disasters, such as civil wars or persecution, where the needs of victims are not necessarily aligned with the strategic interests of the regional big brother.

There is still a lot to be said for a global, multilateral humanitarian regime, led by the UN, particularly if that global regime manages to shed its Western dominance—not only in financing, but also in staffing. Back in 2004, Hugo Slim argued for the need for an 'Ecumenical Humanitarian Council', where representatives of the Western-dominated 'Humanitarian International' (in Alex de Waal's memorable phrase) could meet, talk and agree with new humanitarian actors, such as a resurgent Islamic humanitarianism (Slim, 2004). Since then, emerging humanitarian donors have become more influential and assertive, but the dialogue has often been one of recriminations and distrust. India would be well placed to contribute to placing this 'ecumenical' dialogue on a more constructive track. Its humanitarian track record, and its ability to anchor cosmopolitan humanitarian principles in its own religious and philosophical values, shows that the international humanitarian regime need not be Western-biased, either in theory or in practice.

Funding

The research underpinning this article was funded by the Economic and Social Research Council's Global Uncertainties Fellowship Scheme.

Notes

1. A graphic overview of the European Commission's humanitarian assistance in the aftermath of the 2004 Indian Ocean tsunami can be found at http://ec.europa.eu/echo/files/map/20141217_ECHO_2004-2014_Indian_Ocean_Tsunami.png, accessed 15 April 2015.
2. Bass (2013) provides a vivid account of this fraught relationship between the Indian government and the US Administration during the 1971 war in East Pakistan.
3. The Global Humanitarian Assistance website provides an overview of India's humanitarian contributions, http://www.globalhumanitarianassistance.org/countryprofile/india#tab-home, accessed 15 April 2015.
4. This article was written before India's large-scale relief effort in the aftermath of the Nepal earthquake of 25 April 2015. The Indian relief effort was significant in its size and reach, but also in the debate it engendered in both Nepali and Indian media of perceived Indian high-handedness towards the Nepali government and victims.

References

Anderson, K. (2004) Humanitarian inviolability in crisis: the meaning of impartiality and neutrality for U.N. and NGO agencies following the 2003–2004 Afghanistan and Iraq conflicts, *Harvard Human Rights Journal*, 17, pp. 41–74.

Bass, G. (2013) *The Blood Telegram: Nixon, Kissinger and a Forgotten Genocide*. London: Hurst.

Chanana, D. (2009) India as an emerging donor, *Economic and Political Weekly*, 21 March, 44(12), pp. 11–14.

Cole, T. (2012) The white-savior industrial complex, *The Atlantic*, 21 March, http://www.theatlantic.com/international/archive/2012/03/the-white-savior-industrial-complex/254843/, accessed 17 April 2015.

Das, G. (2009) *The Difficulty of Being Good: On the Subtle Art of Dharma*. Delhi: Penguin Books India.

THE COMMONWEALTH AND THE EUROPEAN UNION IN THE 21ST CENTURY

De Waal, A. (1997) *Famine Crimes: Politics and the Disaster Relief Industry in Africa.* Oxford: James Currey.

ECHO (2005) *Humanitarian Aid Decision 23 02 01,* Document No. ECHO/AS/BUD/2005/02000, Brussels, 16 February.

Economic Times (2015) India has right to attend UNSC decisions on peacekeeping operations, Dalbir Singh Suhag, *The Economic Times,* New Delhi, 28 March, http://articles.economictimes.indiatimes.com/2015-03-28/news/60578855_1_future-peacekeeping-peacekeeping-mandates-dalbir-singh-suhag, accessed 31 March 2015.

Economist (2011) New sources of aid: charity begins abroad, *Economist Magazine,* 13 August.

Economist (2013) The Commonwealth: what is it for?, *Economist Magazine,* 16 November.

Hall, I. (2013) Tilting at windmills? The Indian debate over the responsibility to protect after UNSC Resolution 1973, *Global Responsibility to Protect,* 5, pp. 84–108.

Hammerstad, A. (2012) The Nordics, the EU and Africa, in A. Adebajo and K. Whiteman (Eds), *The EU and Africa: From Eurafrique to Afro-Europa.* London: Hurst.

Hammerstad, A. (2014) *The Rise and Decline of a Global Security Actor: UNHCR, Refugee Protection and Security* Oxford: Oxford University Press.

Indian Development Cooperation Research (2015a) *50 Years of Indian Technical and Economic Cooperation: A Report.* New Delhi: Indian Development Cooperation Research, Centre for Policy Research, January.

Indian Development Cooperation Research (2015b) *Indian Development Assistance: Budget Brief: Trends in 2014–15.* New Delhi: Indian Development Cooperation Research, Centre for Policy Research, February.

Kreling, B. (2009) India and the Commonwealth: a symbiotic relationship?, *The Round Table,* 98(400), pp. 49–66.

Meier, C. and Murthy, C. S. R. (2011) India's Growing Involvement in Humanitarian Assistance, *GPPi Research Paper No. 13.* Berlin: Global Public Policy Institute, January.

Ministry of External Affairs (2005a) *Bridging the Ocean: India Leads Relief Efforts in Tsunami-hit Areas, December 2004–January 2005, Report by the External Publicity Division.* New Delhi: MEA, January.

Ministry of External Affairs (2005b) Joint Media Briefing by Foreign Secretary Shri Shyam Saran and Vice Admiral Shri Raman Puri, Chief of Integrated Service Command. New Delhi: MEA, 5 January, http://www.mea.gov.in/media-briefings.htm?dtl/3470/Joint+Media+Briefing+by+Foreign+Secretary+Shri+Shyam+Saran+and+Vice+Admiral+Shri+Raman+Puri+Chief+of+Integrated+Service+Command, accessed 31 March 2015.

Ministry of External Affairs (2013) *India and the Commonwealth.* Delhi: MEA, October.

Ministry of External Affairs (n.d. [2014/15]) *Indian Diplomacy at Work: Our View: UN Security Council Reforms.* Delhi: MEA.

Modi, N. (2014) Statement by H. E. Narendra Modi, Prime Minister of India, *General Debate of the 69th Session of the United Nations General Assembly,* New York, 27 September.

Organisation for Economic Cooperation and Development (2014) *Active With India.* Paris: OECD, November.

Price, G. (2005) Diversity in Donorship: The Changing Landscape of Official Humanitarian Aid: India's Official Aid Programme, *HGP Background Paper.* London: Overseas Development Institute, September.

Quadir, F. (2013) Rising donors and the new narrative of 'South–South' cooperation: what prospects for changing the landscape of development assistance programmes?, *Third World Quarterly,* 34(2), pp. 321–338.

Roche, E. (2012) India goes from aid beneficiary to donor, *Mint newspaper,* 1 July, http://www.livemint.com/Politics/BToxm8wd11xe45wSBbkqGO/India-goes-from-aid-beneficiary-to-donor.html, accessed 31 March 2015.

Slim, H. (2004) *How We Look: Hostile Perceptions of Humanitarian Action.* Geneva: Centre for Humanitarian Dialogue.

United Nations Development and Planning Organisation (2014) *Background Note: United Nations Peacekeeping, DPI/2429/Rev.18.* New York: UN, April.

United Nations High Commissioner for Refugees (2014) *UNHCR Global Report 2013.* Geneva: UNHCR.

The European Union in Sudan: A Missed Opportunity?

GORDON D. CUMMING
Cardiff University, Cardiff, UK

ABSTRACT *International organisations active in Africa are often criticised for their ineffectiveness. So too is the European Union (EU), which is also accused of failing to assume a more prominent conflict management role in war-torn countries. This article examines the EU's capacity and readiness to take on such a role in one such country, the former Republic of Sudan, home to Africa's longest-running civil wars and the first 'genocide' of the 21st century. It begins by outlining the EU's record in Darfur and the North–South Peace Process. Drawing upon 25 interviews and Hill's 'capabilities–expectations model', it then questions whether the EU's 'capabilities' (resources, instruments, unity) were 'fit for purpose' in Sudan's hostile target setting. It concludes by identifying settings that have been more propitious for a conflict-related management function and by suggesting that the EU should better manage expectations about future security roles.*

Introduction

International organisations operating in Africa are often subject to criticism. The Commonwealth and United Nations (UN), for example, are regularly accused of being ineffective, indecisive and even irrelevant (Knight, 2000; Watkins, 2014). While the European Union (EU) is also criticised on these grounds, it is perhaps more commonly belittled for 'punching below its weight' (Thomas, 2012) and failing to assume a more high-profile conflict management role in war-torn countries (Williams and Bellamy, 2005; Olsen, 2009).[1]

This article examines the EU's capacity and readiness to act as a conflict manager in one such country, the former Republic of Sudan (1956–2011), home to Africa's longest-running civil wars (1955–72, 1983–2005) and to the first 'genocide' of the 21st century, in Sudan's western province, Darfur. It asks whether the EU missed chances to take on a prominent conflict-related role in Sudan or whether, with its nascent common security and defence policy (CSDP) and faced with a hostile Sudanese context, the EU was simply not in a strong enough position to assume such a function.

This question is at the heart of this research, which is significant in two main ways. First, it provides a fresh perspective on what Christopher Hill (1993, 1998) has called

---

This is an Open Access article distributed under the terms of the Creative Commons Attribution License (http://creativecommons.org/licenses/by/4.0/), which permits unrestricted use, distribution, and reproduction in any medium, provided the original work is properly cited.

the 'capabilities–expectations gap' by viewing this through the prism of contexts or 'target settings', taken here to refer to the empirical reality on the ground. Second, it sheds new light on the way that the EU dealt with major challenges facing Sudan over an extended period. In so doing, it makes a meaningful contribution to the existing literature, which has tended to focus more narrowly on the EU's response to the Darfur Crisis: its role in supporting the African Union (AU) mission in Sudan's western province (International Crisis Group (ICG), 2005), its policy on conflict mediation (Middleton *et al.*, 2011) and its failure to intervene militarily in Darfur (Williams and Bellamy, 2005; Toje, 2008; Gya, 2010).

To answer the above research question, this article makes use of Hill's (1993, 1998) 'capabilities–expectations model', which identifies the future functions that the EU as a foreign policy actor might be expected to fulfil, and examines its capabilities (in the form of resources, instruments and unity) to meet these expectations. It sets out the EU's record in Sudan from the time of the Darfur Crisis in 2003 through to the North–South Peace Process culminating in the 2011 referendum, with brief consideration also being given to subsequent developments in the states that emerged from that referendum: Sudan and South Sudan. Drawing upon 25 interviews in Khartoum, London, Paris and Brussels, it then explains this record in terms of the 'fitness for purpose' of the EU's capabilities for Sudan's hostile target setting. It concludes by identifying settings that have been more propitious for a conflict-related management function and by suggesting that the EU should better manage expectations about future security roles.

Research Focus and Methodology

Before proceeding, it is worth sharpening the research focus. First, the emphasis here is primarily on the EU and its institutions rather than on individual European member states. While it is hard to disentangle the two, the role of the latter will be largely confined to our analysis of 'unity' within the EU. Second, the main focus is on two key aspects of the Sudanese case, namely the Darfur Crisis as from 2003 and the North–South Peace Process as from the signature of the Comprehensive Peace Agreement (CPA) in 2005. Space constraints do not allow for discussion of the whole gamut of Sudanese disputes over the last decade and a half, whether in the East, the 'Three Areas' (Nuba Mountains, Southern Blue Nile and Abyei), or indeed between different ethnic factions in the new state of South Sudan (ICG, 2015).

Third, this article does not assume that the EU should necessarily be 'raising its flag' (Hazelzet, 2006, p. 569), enhancing its 'actorness',[2] or strengthening its 'presence'. Indeed, there may be good reasons for the EU not to raise its profile (taken here to equate to 'image' or 'standing'), particularly if that helps 'get the job done' (Hazelzet, 2006, p. 569) or if it creates space for 'coordinated bilateral diplomatic efforts by EU member states' (Vines, 2010, p. 1,091).

Finally, my intention is not to develop a new theory or even an alternative to Hill's model, which has survived, relatively unscathed, in the fast-moving world of international relations.[3] Instead, my aim is to apply the model in a more nuanced way by viewing the EU's 'capabilities' through the prism of specific 'target settings' and by giving greater consideration to ways in which the EU manages 'expectations'. On the first point, there will clearly need to be some discussion of the wider context, or what

THE COMMONWEALTH AND THE EUROPEAN UNION IN THE 21ST CENTURY

Bretherton and Vogel (2006) term 'the opportunity structure'. However, the real emphasis here will be on the target setting, that is, the reality on the ground, and the way that these 'local' political, geographical and strategic factors affect the EU's 'fitness for purpose' for particular challenges.

On the second point, regarding expectations, word limits do not allow for consideration of whether Hill's (1993, pp. 312–315) predictions about future EU roles have held true. Such an analysis would no doubt reveal that the EU nowadays is not a 'superpower' (a position reserved for the US and increasingly China), a 'global intervenor' (as its limited influence in the Israeli–Palestinian dispute demonstrates), or indeed a 'mediator of conflicts' (as shown by its inability to secure a place on the Mbeki Panel, discussed later). The EU has arguably fared better as a 'bridge between rich and poor' (the EU is the world's largest donor), 'regional pacifier' (the EU has played an important role in stabilising the Balkans) and 'joint supervisor of the world economy' (the EU is a major player in World Trade Organisation) (Toje, 2008, pp. 138–139). Whatever the findings of future research on this topic, the key point to emphasise here is that expectations regarding the EU's role as a conflict manager have remained high, particularly among the public, in most European countries (interview with European Institute of Security Studies, January 2012). This is perhaps not surprising considering some of the statements issued by the EU. A case in point was the 2003 European Security Strategy ('A Secure Europe in a Better World'), which stressed the 'need to develop a strategic culture that fosters early, rapid and when necessary, robust intervention'. Nor is it particularly remarkable given that a 'strong focus on ... conflict management is ... exactly in line with crucial values and ideas that contribute to the EU's identity' and is consistent with its 'goal of turning the Union into a significant international actor' (Olsen, 2007, p. 12).

The EU's Record in Sudan

The European Community (EC)/EU had little chance to play a visible role in Sudan over the early post-colonial era. Before even achieving independence in 1956, this former Anglo-Egyptian condominium had lapsed into the first of two protracted civil wars. The EU's profile in Sudan was further reduced when, in March 1990, it suspended development assistance, expressing concern about the recent military coup and human rights violations. This suspension put EU–Sudanese relations formally on hold for over a decade, even if the EU did manage to channel €450 million in humanitarian assistance between 1992 and 2002 (European Commission, 2005, p. 14).

It was not, however, until November 1999 that relations began to thaw. In recognition of progress made by the Sudanese government and the Sudanese Popular Liberation Movement/Army (SPLM/SPLA: John Garang's southern political group) towards a peace agreement, the EU began a formal political dialogue with the regime in Khartoum. By January 2002, following progress in these talks, the EU had launched the Humanitarian Plus programme providing monies for rehabilitation-related activities.

Darfur Crisis

It was then against this backdrop of improved EU–Sudanese relations that fighting erupted in March 2003 in the Darfur region between government forces and rebels from the Sudan Liberation Army (SLA) and the Justice and Equality Movement (JEM). On the face of it, the Darfur Crisis presented the EU with a real opportunity to go beyond dialogue and establish itself in a conflict management capacity. In this context, Williams and Bellamy (2005) have contended that the EU was one of the few actors that could have intervened militarily, while Toje (2008, p. 135) has claimed that 'With the UN deadlocked, and having declared the European Security and Defence policy (ESDP) operational just one month' earlier, the EU was 'always the most likely candidate to carry out such a mission', not least since Darfur was 'exactly the sort of question that the ESDP was created to handle', as it fell 'within the narrow confines of where the EU states have agreed that the use of force can be necessary'.

By mid-2004 there were indeed signs that a military option was being considered by the EU, whose top military official, Gustav Hagglund, affirmed that this was 'very possible' (Channel News Asia, 12 April 2004). In July, British Prime Minister Tony Blair stressed that he was 'ruling nothing out', while UK Foreign Secretary Jack Straw revealed that Britain and its EU partners were discussing the despatch of 'a joint EU civilian and military team', which might include troop deployments (*The Daily Telegraph*, 23 July 2004). In August, Blair suggested the UK had a 'moral responsibility' to help and placed 5,000 troops on standby (Williams, 2006, p. 172). The following month saw US Secretary of State Colin Powell opening the door to military intervention—though not by the US—by labelling the killings in Darfur 'genocide'. By December, however, the number UK troops on standby had fallen to 3,000 (Agence France Presse, 26 December 2004) and by June 2005 the UK government was emphasising that it had 'no plans to send UK troops to Darfur' (Williams, 2006, p. 172). The UK's backtracking reflected its concerns over British military overstretch, NATO's reluctance to become involved other than in a support capacity (BBC, 2005), the opposition by Russia and China to any intervention without a firm UN mandate, the concern of smaller EU member states to find alternative options, and France's unwillingness to 'shoulder a significant part of the burden' or to 'support coercive measures' (Toje, 2008, p. 137).

Thereafter the EU, while not abandoning its quest for visibility, fell into a supporting role. One aspect of this involved backing non-EU civilian–military missions. In this context, the EU became the main funder of AMIS, an AU observer mission deployed in June 2004 to monitor compliance with the N'Djamena ceasefire agreed two months earlier. Recognising the mission's lack of capacity to operate in such a hostile region, the EU helped to transform AMIS into AMIS II in October, thereby allowing the enhancement of the African force with more troops, including a civilian police component. But the shortcomings of AMIS II soon became equally apparent, and the EU joined other northern donors in pressing Khartoum to accept a successor mission, UNAMID. Authorised by the UN Security Council (UNSC) in July 2007, UNAMID was a hybrid force involving the AU and UN and designed to include 19,000 troops and 3,700 civilian personnel (Reuters, 13 June 2007). Three EU member states—Britain, France and Sweden—contributed a small number of military personnel, while several others provided civilian police officers (Gya, 2010, pp. 12–13).

Another feature of the EU's supporting role was sanctions. Thus, the EU backed UNSC resolutions (1,556 in 2004 and 1,591 in 2005), which placed arms embargoes on non-state actors operating in Darfur. In 2005, it also imposed autonomous sanctions on the Sudanese government (Sicurelli, 2010, p. 67). These included restrictions on admission and freezing the funds of targeted individuals. Thereafter, the EU was a key supporter of the indictments, issued in March 2009 and July 2010, by the International Criminal Court (ICC) against Sudan's sitting head of state, President Omar al-Bashir. It called upon the Sudanese government to respect this ruling and publicly criticised states refusing to arrest Bashir on their soil.

A final dimension of the EU's back-up function involved conflict mediation. Here, the EU sought to carve out a role for itself by assigning a special envoy, Sten Rylander, to assist with peace negotiations on Darfur. In July 2005, it raised its profile by appointing an EU Special Representative (EUSR), Pekko Haavisto, to 'achieve a political settlement in Darfur' (Middleton *et al.*, 2011, p. 19). Haavisto was then 'heavily involved in mediating' what was a 'rushed and badly organized process' (Middleton *et al.*, 2011, p. 21) that led to the failed 2006 Darfur Peace Agreement in Abuja. The next EUSR, Torben Brylle, played a lower key role, sitting in on the joint AU–UN mediation talks in Doha from 2007 (Middleton *et al.*, 2011). The EUSR from 2010–13, Dame Rosalind Marsden, also engaged in the Doha talks and, as one of the E6 (envoys from the EU, UK, US, France, Russia, China, who first met in May 2009), played a part in ensuring that Doha was not eclipsed by Darfuri mediation processes and that it brought about the signature of the Doha Document for Peace in Darfur in July 2011 (interview with Nordic official, Brussels, June 2013). To this day, however, fighting has continued in Darfur, with Darfuri rebels now forming, together with northern-based SPLA units, a broad anti-Khartoum coalition known as the Sudan Revolutionary Front (ICG, 2015, p. 1).

The North–South Peace Process

Turning to the North–South Peace Process, this was of course going on at the same time as the Darfur Crisis, even if donors generally sought to keep the issues separate and often prioritised the former (interview with French official, Khartoum, May 2010). The peace negotiations made headway in the early 2000s with the signing of protocols (on wealth-sharing, power-sharing, security and the Three Areas), which, taken together, constituted the CPA. The CPA was a six-year roadmap for peace, granting the South a degree of autonomy, promising elections and a referendum on secession, and establishing a UN mission (UNMIS) to monitor the ceasefire. The agreement was signed in Naivasha in January 2005 by Sudan's government and the SPLM, as part of a regional (Intergovernmental Authority for Development or IGAD-led) process, reinforced by international observers. Yet while the EU had not sent a special envoy to the negotiations, it was invited to 'guarantee' the CPA and sit on the Assessment and Evaluation Commission (AEC), which monitored the implementation of the CPA.[4] The EU's invitation to the top table did not, however, imply that it was being taken seriously by other AEC members (the US, Norway, UK, Holland and Italy). Rather, as one Nordic official explained: 'It was accepted that it was more useful to have the EU round the table in an observer role because of its large donor commitment and its coordinating function, more on the donor than the political side' (interview in Brussels, June 2013).

Rather than force its way into the foreground, the EU dutifully implemented the terms of an agreement that had been crafted by other, more influential players. Thus, in 2005, the European Commission produced a Country Strategy Paper, offering a comprehensive €400 million development assistance package aimed at supporting stability, education, food security, peace-building, demobilisation, disarmament and reintegration operations (European Commission, 2005, p. 3).

While the EU continued in this back-seat role over the next five years, it nonetheless had opportunities to raise its profile, notably at the time of the April 2010 elections, the January 2011 referendum and in the early post-referendum period. In the case of the elections, the EU provided technical and logistical support, co-chaired (with Holland and the UK) the UN Development Programme-managed election basket-fund, and contributed €12.5 million to it (Middleton *et al.*, 2011, p. 21). The EU also impressed on the Sudanese government the importance of 'an open political space' (interview with EUSR, Brussels, November 2011), as well as sending a huge election observer mission. As regards the referendum on the secession of South Sudan, here too the EU played a visible role. It contributed €3.25 million to the UN Development Programme referendum basket-fund (Middleton *et al.*, 2011, p. 21). It also deployed long-term observers in Sudan from November 2010 as well as a large observer mission in January 2011.

In the wake of the referendum, which resulted, six months later, in the inauguration of Africa's 54th state, South Sudan, the EU had a unique opportunity to raise its profile as a conflict manager and mediator. Against a backdrop of continuing North–Sudan disputes and growing violence in Abyei, South Kordofan and the Blue Niles States (ICG, 2015), the EU adopted a 'Comprehensive Approach', which was supposed to allow it to mobilise all the instruments at its disposal in support of 'peace, justice and democratisation' (personal communication, European External Action Service (EEAS), November 2011). In line with this approach, the EU launched, in June 2012, an 18-month CSDP civilian mission (EUAVSEC) to bolster airport security in Juba, South Sudan. It did, however, have to shelve other potential operations—a medium-term border policing mission and a longer-term patrol of the Nile (Bloch, 2011)—following the outbreak of civil war in South Sudan in December 2013.

The EU was also beset by problems in its attempts to establish its credentials as a conflict mediator. Believing that Thabo Mbeki had privileged access both to President Bashir and to South Sudan's President Salva Kiir (Zwan, 2011, p. 18), the EU invested heavily in the (Mbeki-led) AU High-level Implementation Panel, which was charged with resolving outstanding CPA and post-CPA issues. It provided the bulk of the funding and even offered three technical experts. However, two of these experts were subsequently declined (on nationality grounds), as was a request from the EU High Representative Baroness Catherine Ashton that the EUSR should participate in the work of the panel (Middleton *et al.*, 2011, p. 20).[5]

Faced with these setbacks, the EU has, unsurprisingly, sought to foreground its developmental rather than conflict management role, particularly in South Sudan. It transformed its sub-office into a full embassy in Juba in May 2011 and, in June, began a joint programming process, whereby the EU coordinates the bilateral aid efforts of its member states. However, the EU's actions have been constrained by two recent developments. The first was South Sudan's refusal to sign the Cotonou Agreement—Europe's aid and trade convention with former African, Caribbean and Pacific colonies—for fear of SPLM figures being indicted by the ICC (Olsen and Furness, 2014, p. 10). The second was the outbreak, in December 2013, of large-scale fighting between President Kiir's Dinka community and Vice-President Riek Machar's Nuer supporters. The EU delegation has now largely suspended its long-term development programmes and gone back to concentrating on humanitarian assistance (Olsen and Furness, 2014).

EU Capabilities: 'Fitness for Purpose'

It follows that the EU did not carve out a high-profile conflict management role either in Darfur or during the North–South Peace Process. In part, this can be explained by a lack of political will but in part it is also linked to the 'fitness for purpose' of the EU's 'capabilities' (resources, instruments and unity) for raising its profile in this target setting.

Resources

The EU has had vast resources to spend on Sudan. Indeed, 'EC aid to the Sudan jumped by ... 1000 per cent from 2001 to 2005' (Olsen, 2007, p. 13). With the signing of the CPA in 2005, the EU promised a €400 million development assistance package and continued providing €100 million annually in humanitarian assistance (personal communication, EEAS, November 2011). The EU maintained flows of development assistance even after the Bashir government refused, in July 2009, to ratify the Cotonou Agreement, potentially turning its back on €336 million pledged under the 10th European Development Fund (EDF) (Olsen, 2007, p. 13). Significantly too, the EU remained the second largest donor to the Multi Donor Trust Fund-South Sudan, while European member states continued to pay more than 40% of the costs of UNMIS and UNAMID (Zwan, 2011, p. 19).

The above 'soft power' resources were enough to secure the EU a place at most top tables. But they afforded only limited leverage in a target setting such as Sudan, where oil revenues were high (Patey, 2007) and where the regime in Khartoum had no interest in resolving humanitarian crises, even going so far as to expel, in March 2009, 16 relief agencies operating in Darfur (IRIN, 2009).

As regards 'human resources', EU staff operating in Sudan displayed 'a bit of inexperience on the political side' (interview with European official, Khartoum, May 2010). They were more comfortable dealing with technical development issues than strategic questions and, when the European Commission was charged with chairing the N'Djamena ceasefire monitoring commission, they had to rely entirely on member states for military advice (ICG, 2005, p. 10).

The same cannot be said of the EUSRs, who were much more politically astute. However, these envoys did not all attach the same importance to raising the EU's profile. The first EUSR was 'the politically proactive and independent Haavisto [who] failed to acknowledge the limits of his mandate' (Ferhatović, n.d., p. 7). He was succeeded in 2007 by Danish diplomat Torben Brylle, 'who respected the limitations set by leading member states', but was widely regarded as an observer and who never actually met the Sudanese president (interview with Whitehall insider, June 2013). The next EUSR, Marsden, was highly respected, even if her appointment in August 2010 was problematic in the eyes of some European ambassadors in Khartoum given that she had just been UK High Commissioner (interviews, May 2010). In the end, all these EUSRs were hampered by the fact that their advisors were seconded for short periods by member states, were thought to 'remain loyal to the seconding structures that pay their salaries' (Ferhatović 2009, p. 51) and were not in post long enough to move beyond a 'reactive approach to conflict management' (Zwan, 2011, p. 22).

THE COMMONWEALTH AND THE EUROPEAN UNION IN THE 21ST CENTURY

Instruments

Turning to instruments, here the EU has also had a vast array of tools with which to assume a more prominent conflict-related role. To begin with CSDP military missions, these are arguably the EU's most conspicuous instrument, offering the immediate prospect of enhanced visibility. However, as noted earlier, the EU failed to launch an operation in Darfur, and the explanation for this lies at least partly in the target setting in Sudan, where a brutal regime, backed by China and Russia, was resisting any international military engagement. By contrast, the EU's subsequent success in undertaking a civilian CSDP mission (EUAVSEC, 2012) in Juba can also be understood in terms of changes in the target setting: South Sudan was a new state, which desperately needed to boost its trade, regionally and internationally, and whose leaders had long been pushing for an operation of this kind (interview with EUSR advisor, January 2012).

The EU's other conflict management tools were more low-key, often serving to support other actors. To illustrate, the EU contributed €3 million, via its Instrument for Stability (IFS), to the trust fund that finances the AU–UN-led peace process in Darfur (House of Lords, 2011, p. 42).[6] Similarly, the EU made contributions to the AMIS and UNAMID missions. While these were more sizeable (some €440 million between 2004 and 2007 and over 100 military personnel (confidential personal communication, EEAS, November 2011)), they did not raise the EU's profile in Sudan for several reasons. First, AMIS was under-resourced and had no established mediation capacity (ICG, 2005). Second, it was financed by the Africa Peace Facility (APF), which is itself funded by the EDF and hence precludes expenditure on military equipment. Finally, in the case of UNAMID, the EU was only allowed to supply a tiny number of military personnel and was subsequently required by the Sudanese government to withdraw all of them (interview with defence attaché, Khartoum, May 2010).

Another measure that could have marked the EU out as a serious player was sanctions. However, in practice, the EU hid behind the UN on arms embargoes and adopted economic sanctions that were 'less restrictive than those imposed by the US' (Sicurelli, 2010, pp. 49, 67). The EU's reticence was largely the result of a lack of political will but also reflected a recognition that sanctions were unlikely to sway an oil-rich Sudanese regime and might even afford other players greater influence at a point in the peace process when the EU had to remain engaged (interview with former EUSR advisor, Brussels, January 2012). The precedent for this had already been set in the 1990s when 'Western' sanctions had allowed China, Malaysia and India to become the dominant investors in Sudan's oil sector (Patey, 2007, p. 5).

The same reticence did not mark the EU's approach to the ICC's 2009 indictment as it soon became the donor that was most systematic in refusing to meet Bashir. However, the ICC was a double-edged sword. As one EUSR advisor made clear: 'The EU is perceived as a strong actor by sticking to its principles. But this ties our hands politically. We can't engage with Bashir. The AU is also very "anti" the ICC Resolution. Paradoxically, every time Bashir travels to another country, our influence diminishes' (interview in Brussels, November 2011). In practice, this self-denying ordinance meant that the EU was excluded from high-level negotiations with the president and had to find other interlocutors. According to one EEAS official (interview in Brussels, 2012), 'these could be Heads of State within the region' or 'the circle around the president' who 'then pass on messages'. The ultimate irony of the EU's principled stand is that the continuing threat of arrest by the ICC is now the main obstacle to Bashir stepping down and opening the door to meaningful national dialogue (Confidential communication, London, July 2015).

Other EU instruments have included missions to observe the elections and referendums. While these were high-profile, their findings were never going to be allowed to derail the North-South peace process. They also exposed the EU to criticism. The EU was accused of 'losing momentum in the period building up to the referendum' (interview with Nordic official, June 2013) and, before the elections themselves, of arriving too late for the original census, by which time much rigging had already been done. According to one election advisor (interview in Khartoum, May 2010):

> The Carter Center had been on the ground with four teams since February 2008. We were pushing the EU to have its observers on the ground in time for voter registration starting on 1 November. Brussels is non-functional in summer. If you want to be a major player here, you can't take the summer off.

Finally, another soft power instrument was EU declarations. These were arguably the EU's preferred approach but had no obvious impact on the Khartoum regime. On leaving office, the Finnish EUSR Haavisto commented on the futility of the EU expressing, for the 54th time, 'verbal concern' about the situation on the ground in Darfur (*EU Observer*, 1 May 2007).

Unity

Turning to the question of unity, the following analysis will argue that, while there were disagreements between European member states that reduced the EU's prospects of assuming a more prominent EU conflict management role, there was also a 'basic underlying unity' (interview with American diplomat, Khartoum, May 2010) that enabled the EU to play a low-key but vital supporting function.

The clearest example of disunity was over the possible CSDP military mission to Darfur. This is not surprising given that this is where the EU is most dependent on member states for military contributions and 'political direction' (Gya, 2010, p. 12). Crucially, the EU3 (Germany, the UK and France), whose agreement is usually required to launch an operation, were not united (Toje, 2008, p. 135). Germany, which is never an enthusiastic supporter of such missions (interview with French Foreign Ministry, November 2011), was seeking alternatives. The UK favoured a NATO lead, while France opposed this (Sicurelli, 2010, p. 61). The fact that Britain and France were supposed to be cooperating more closely in line with the 1998 St Malo II Agreement was ignored by the UK, which jealously guarded its status as part of the Troika (Norway, US, UK), the most influential northern players in Sudan.

Other disagreements were much less in the public spotlight. There were, for example, divergences over the EU's support for AMIS, with some member states pushing for APF funds to be used to finance this mission, while others saw this as a '"slippery slope", with development funds being increasingly called upon to fund military work' (Olsen, 2007, p. 10).

Equally, there were differences over the ICC indictment. While this was supported rhetorically across the EU, whose members had all signed the Rome Statute on which the ICC was founded, member states had different interpretations of what was meant by 'essential contact'. The Dutch took the toughest line, with their ambassador even absenting himself from Bashir's swearing-in ceremony in 2010, while the UK adopted a more relaxed stance: the British High Commissioner paid her respects when leaving office (interviews with Whitehall insider, June 2013). As a rule, AEC member states were keenest to leave channels open to Bashir. As one of their officials explained: 'If you want to push implementation of the CPA, you need to leave [a] door open to the different parties—SPLM and [the government's] National Congress Party' (interview, Khartoum, May 2010).

Other disputes were kept even further out of public view. These included disagreements over who should pay the cost of transporting ballot papers from Khartoum to Juba, then on to polling stations. Some member states argued that this was the responsibility of Sudan's electoral commission but AEC members pushed the EU to make these payments, which they eventually did (interviews, Khartoum, May 2010). More significantly, there were 'different sensibilities' on how rigorously the EU should judge the 2010 electoral process, with 'the Dutch at the hard end, the UK much softer and the EU somewhere in the middle' (interview with Whitehall insider, June 2013). According to one European official (interview in Khartoum, May 2010), 'Nobody in the EU disputed the criticisms by the observer mission. But ultimately the election was needed for the CPA. In the end, we all signed up to … semi-credible, D-minus elections'.

Finally, there were even differences over EU declarations. According to one European official (interview in Khartoum, May 2010), 'Some countries such as Sweden and Romania were pushing for declarations' as a way for them 'to be visible'. Others, such as the UK, preferred to 'go it alone on a declaration unless it [was] a very controversial thing'. They would 'then ask for the cover of the EU and … share the blame with others'.

The above analysis certainly suggests disunity, with 'bilateral donors all feel[ing] that they need to be seen or heard', 'all wanting to claim success' and some preferring 'a bilateral approach to the North–South dialogue and Darfur' rather than 'stronger coordination by the EUSR' (Zwan, 2011, p. 24). Ultimately, however, many of the differences should not be overstated as they were less about interests (discussed later) than divergent norms (House of Lords, 2011, p. 116). These included differences over the order of priority in which different Sudanese challenges should be tackled. According to one Whitehall insider (interview, June 2013), there was a 'division between the EU, whose focus was on Darfur especially under Brylle, and growing concern in London and Holland about the North–South process and drift on the CPA'. As the same interviewee made clear: 'The issue was not so much a lack of consensus since everyone was broadly agreed on the need for peace, democratic transition and fair and free elections. But there were different perspectives on norms and pace and who got the credit for state-building'. This point was reinforced by an American diplomat (interview in Khartoum, May 2010), who noted that EU positions displayed 'a lot of crucial common ground': on the priority attached to CPA, the need to move towards democracy, and the importance of the referendum. This underlying unity was linked to a fear of doing anything that might derail the peace process. In this sense, Sudan's hostile target setting appears actually to have facilitated difficult compromises and made it easier for the EU to assume a low-key supporting role.

THE COMMONWEALTH AND THE EUROPEAN UNION IN THE 21ST CENTURY

Target Setting

The above analysis has shown how, despite having a range of resources, an array of instruments and a degree of unity, the EU has been unable to carve out a high-profile conflict management role. The explanation for this lies at least partly in the target setting in Sudan. In other words, it may be questioned whether the Sudanese context was ever really propitious for a CSDP military mission. Was it the kind of place that the EU might have been expected to emerge as a power broker or might the EU have done better to reframe expectations?

Before homing in on this setting, it is worth remembering that EU–Sudanese relations were playing out in a wider context or 'opportunity structure' (Bretheron and Vogel, 2006). This external environment was clearly important in establishing the tone of these relations and, as such, some of its key features are outlined below. At the risk of over-simplifying, the early 2000s can be said to have offered a favourable climate for a more prominent EU conflict management role. In December 2001, the EU had declared its rapid reaction force (50,000–60,000 troops available at 60 days' notice) to be operational. In June 2003, the EU launched the first CSDP mission in Africa and, in December, adopted the European Security Strategy. Equally, European leaders at this time, notably Tony Blair and French President Jacques Chirac, were prepared to invest in an interventionist strategy towards Africa. They were aided in this by support from civil society groups across Europe, keen to ram home the lessons of the Rwandan genocide, as well by growing acceptance of the right of states to intervene in line with the UN's Responsibility to Protect doctrine (Williams and Bellamy, 2005).

By the end of the North–South Peace Process, the EU was institutionally better equipped to take on a conflict management role. It had ratified the 2007 Lisbon Treaty, established the EEAS in 2010, introduced two EU–Africa strategies (2005, 2007) plus specific strategies for the Sahel and Horn (2011), as well as issuing a joint communication on the 'Comprehensive Approach' in 2013 (European Commission/High Representative, 2013). At the same time, however, the EU was in the grip of a major global recession, its leaders were wary of CSDP military missions—having been press-ganged by France into European Force (EUFOR) Chad in 2008—and the UK's Conservative Prime Minister David Cameron was even mooting the possibility of a UK exit from the EU. In addition, Africa had been 'bumped down the agenda by the Arab Spring' and the AU was, in line with the mantra 'African solutions to African problems', pressing harder to take the lead on missions and negotiations across Africa (interview with former EUSR advisor, November 2011, Brussels).

While the international climate may have become less favourable over time, it was not a block on CSDP military missions across much of Africa, as will be seen in the conclusion. So what was it about the target setting in Sudan that curbed the EU's capacity to project itself as a major player in the conflict field, particularly in the period from the 2003 Darfur Crisis to the end of the peace process in 2011? The first factor was the brutality of the Khartoum regime, its unresponsiveness to soft power and its vehement resistance to hard power. In this context, one former EUSR advisor stressed that: 'To do a CSDP mission [in Darfur] without the consent of the government of Sudan was impossible. We needed their consent. We needed a UN Security Council Resolution. The Sudanese regime was blocking our efforts to intervene' (interview in Brussels, January 2012). Another EUSR advisor claimed: 'We were not allowed a logic of European engagement by Khartoum. Was it really a missed opportunity?' (Interview in Brussels, January 2012.)

The second element was the hostility of the physical terrain and the scale of the challenge. Sudan was, until 2011, Africa's largest country, and its Darfur region was the size of France but with no major surfaced road network and dirt tracks that were at the mercy of the summer rains. Furthermore, Sudan was home to multiple significant conflicts, most notably in the East and the Three Areas, not to mention many localised disputes over pasture rights and access to water, that could trigger large-scale conflicts (Zwan, 2011, p. 23). Importantly too, Sudan was a strategic hotspot surrounded by nine neighbouring countries, all of which stood to be affected adversely by any breakdown in the Sudanese peace process. In such a setting, it is hard to see how the EU, which had 'only started getting involved in "crisis management" operations in 1999' (Gya, 2010, p. 10), could have assumed a power broker role or sustained the kind of open-ended interventions that were needed in Darfur and other Sudanese conflict zones. Its chances of doing so would doubtless have been increased by the availability of NATO assets and planning facilities, but NATO's engagement in Sudan would, of course, have been anathema to the Bashir regime.

The third feature was the 'crowdedness' of the political space. Sudan was described by one European ambassador as 'a competitive environment', with a large number of external players pursuing different interests (interview in Khartoum, May 2010). As noted earlier, these actors included emerging powers, such as China and Russia, whose interests centred on oil and arms, respectively (Patey, 2007). The US, with equities across the region, was also heavily involved, as was Norway, with its oil interests. The AU, which 'always wants to run everything' (interview in Khartoum, May 2010), and IGAD were two of the key regional players. The EU arrived late on this scene, even if the UK, the former colonial power with major equities in East Africa and Egypt, as well as Holland and Italy had all been heavily involved in the Naivasha talks. This meant there was competition between individual EU member states and between these states and the EU. According to Middleton *et al.* (2011, p. 24):

> The UK has been the pre-eminent EU member state voice on Sudan and along with the Netherlands has rather crowded out the EU. In a situation where foreign players have tended to adopt areas of specialty (oil for Norway, security for the UK, the Three Areas for the Netherlands) the EU's generalist approach without the hard political clout of the US has led to it finding itself on the sidelines.

This crowding out was sometimes justified on the grounds that it helped channel support to a country which received 'a lot of supply driven assistance' (interview with American diplomat, May 2010). It was also deemed necessary to ensure that the CPA ran its course. Such a competitive approach was, however, harder to defend in post-referendum South Sudan. Yet it continued, as can be seen from the divisions over the EU's adoption of joint programming in Sudan. This approach, which seeks to harmonise the development policies of European member states and minimise the strain on local Sudanese capacity, has been resisted by some EU states, which see it as 'an add-on to their bilateral engagement rather than as an overarching coordination mechanism, and even as a chance to get EU money to support bilateral programmes' (Olsen and

Furness, 2014, p. 8). The UK has been the worst culprit and has, together with the Netherlands, published a detailed country strategy that barely mentions the EU (Olsen and Furness, 2014, pp. 8, 10).

Conclusion: Looking Beyond the Sudanese Case

This article began by noting that international organisations active in Africa frequently face criticism. The EU is no exception and is often accused of missing opportunities to assert itself as a conflict manager. This study asked whether these claims were borne out by the EU's record in Sudan from the time of the Darfur Crisis through to the transition to a two-state solution. It found that there was indeed a lack of political will and quite high levels of disagreement among member states that militated against a more prominent conflict-related role. At the same time, however, it questioned whether the EU had really missed chances to undertake CSDP military missions or emerge as a power broker. It suggested that, while the EU did have a range of resources, an array of instruments and a reasonable degree of unity on fundamental issues, it was always going to struggle to translate these 'capabilities' into actual 'muscle' in a target setting as hostile as Sudan.

The above conclusions are not intended to absolve the EU of responsibility for not trying harder to surmount the obstacles it faced in Sudan. They do, however, help to relativise criticisms of the EU as well as opening out on to wider questions on settings and expectation management. The first question concerns the influence of target settings on the EU's readiness to take on conflict management roles, specifically CSDP military missions. Several features of these settings affect the prospects of such an intervention taking place. The attitude of an African regime is clearly important. Where the host government has requested support (as in the Democratic Republic of the Congo (DRC) in 2003 and 2006), it is easier for the EU both to muster member state contributions and to secure UNSC authorisation. Where, however, the regime is opposed, this is more problematic, as the case of Libya in 2011 demonstrated, even if the EU did eventually offer military support for humanitarian operations (EUFOR Libya, 2011).

Proximity should, in theory, increase the likelihood of an EU mission, as the EU's interests are often geographically 'closer to home'. This was certainly true of the EU's Operation Atalanta (as from 2008) off the Somali coast. However, proximity can mean the presence of other important actors, who may be wary of interventions (e.g. China and Russia in Libya and Sudan). Urgency, too, should increase the likelihood of a CSDP mission. This was indeed the case in the DRC where Operation Artemis in 2003 halted the killings in eastern Congo. However, this is often not enough, as evidenced by the EU's initial paralysis over Libya in 2011 and the delays in launching its 2013 mission to the Central African Republic (EUFOR RCA).

The scale of the challenge is another crucial element. A mission is more probable if the issue is likely to resolve quickly, as was the case in eastern DRC (2003), the Congolese elections (2006) and to a lesser extent Chad (2008), where the aim was to create the security conditions needed to hand over to a UN force. It is less likely where the challenge is more open-ended (as in Mali), deep-rooted as in Côte d'Ivoire or linked, as it is today in Sudan and South Sudan (ICG, 2015), to a whole series of interrelated disputes.

The key factor is arguably some kind of historical or political connection, with a potential 'lead nation', such as the UK or France. This linkage really takes effect where the mission serves wider EU economic or security interests. The Atalanta operation is a case in point. So too is the naval intervention to intercept migrant smuggler ships from North Africa which has just been agreed by EU foreign and defence ministers (*New York Times*, 18 May 2015). Historical ties can also work where a lead nation is prepared to invest enough energy into persuading other EU states into supplying troops. This was how France ensured the launch of the 2013 EUFOR RCA mission, despite the fact that the EU had virtually no wider strategic interests at stake (Olsen and Furness, 2014, p. 15).

Turning, finally, to the issue of how best to manage expectations, this is the dimension of the Hillian model that is most neglected. There is, of course, a limit to how far the EU can frame expectations in contexts such as Darfur where the US had, by publicly recognising the 'genocide', encouraged speculation about a strong-armed international response.[7] However, expectation management should be easier in other African contexts and would bring EU discourse more into line with the undeniable reality that the EU has, over the last five years, been moving away from a hybrid approach involving military interventions and civilian missions towards one that is heavily skewed towards capacity-building (the European Union's Capacity Building mission or EUCAP Sahel Niger, 2012; EUCAP NESTOR, 2012) and training (the EU's training mission or EUTM Mali, 2013 and EUCAP Sahel Mali, 2014).[8]

The EU has made an important contribution to conflicts across Africa by assuming many of these low-key functions. Despite this, the EU has felt the urge to continue fuelling unrealistic expectations as to its future conflict management roles. The most recent example is the EU's 2013 Joint Communication on its 'comprehensive approach to external conflict and crises'. This includes a promise to 'coordinate and where possible combine the use of a *full range of EU tools and instruments* … to craft a flexible and effective response *during and after the stabilisation phase and in case of risks of conflict*' (European Commission/High Representative, 2013, p. 9, italics added).

It is easy to see why the EU is seeking a 'whole-of-Union' strategy that makes 'its external action more consistent' (European Commission/High Representative, 2013, pp. 2, 12). What is, however, less clear is why the EU has not sought to qualify the 'comprehensiveness' of this approach by laying down specific criteria—geographic, political and logistical—that could trigger 'CSDP missions and operations' (European Commission/High Representative, 2013, p. 9). By tightening up its discourse in this way, the EU would take an important step towards bridging the capabilities–expectations gap. It would discover the benefits of under-promising and over-delivering, while also building more solid foundations on which its future aspirations as a conflict manager could be based. Furthermore, the EU need not be alone in this process. A similar approach could be adopted by other international organisations active in Africa, not least the Commonwealth and the UN, each of which has its own capabilities–expectations gap and each of which has a need to restore its image in the 21st century.

Acknowledgments

This work was supported by the British Academy [LRG45500]. Thanks are also due to Tony Chafer and Peter Woodward for their comments at the start of this project.

THE COMMONWEALTH AND THE EUROPEAN UNION IN THE 21ST CENTURY

Notes

1. This article avoids the broad definition of conflict management employed in some EU circles which includes conflict prevention and crisis management (Sicurelli, 2010) and is closer to Olsen's (2009) definition, which focuses on military missions, mediation and supporting instruments.
2. 'Actorness' refers to the EU's 'capacity to act' (Jupille and Caporaso, 1998, p. 214), while 'presence' equates to 'the ability to exert influence externally' (Bretherton and Vogler, 2006, pp. 24–30).
3. There have, for example, been alternative empirical approaches (Jupille and Caporaso, 1998) and theoretically informed models focusing on preference-formation (Thomas, 2012).
4. Before the Lisbon Treaty, the EU had one chair for the European Commission and one for the presidency/EUSR (interview with EU Delegation, Khartoum, May 2010).
5. By contrast, the US, Norway and UK have roles within this process (Power, 2015).
6. The IFS is a flexible mechanism that funds short-term crisis management responses.
7. The European Parliament only labelled Sudan's actions as 'tantamount to genocide' (Gya, 2010, p. 10).
8. European member states have contributed troops to MINUSAM, the UN force established in northern Mali in April 2013. The Dutch have deployed 450 peacekeepers. Denmark, Sweden, Norway and Finland have also sent troops.

References

BBC (2005) Analysis: Nato's role in Darfur, BBC News, 29 April, http://news.bbc.co.uk/1/hi/world/africa/4498409.stm, accessed 3 March 2015.

Bloch, S. (2011) CSDP and EU mission update, *European Security Review, Briefing 6*. Brussels: ISIS Europe, June/July.

Bretherton, C. and Vogel, J. (2006) *The European Union as Global Actor*, 2nd edn. New York: Routledge.

Commission European (2005) *Sudan: Country Strategy Paper 2005–2007*. Brussels: European Commission.

European Commission/High Representative (2013) Joint communication: the EU's comprehensive approach to external conflict and crises, JOIN (2013) 30 final.

Ferhatović, E. (n.d.) Implementing peace in Sudan, http://www.atlantic-community.org/app/webroot/files/articlepdf/Ferhatovic%20Sudan.pdf, accessed 9 May 2015.

Ferhatović, E. (2009) Implementing peace in Sudan, *Turkish Policy Quarterly*, 8(4), pp. 45–54.

Gya, G. (2010) *The EU's Role in the Darfur Crisis*. Madrid: Fride.

Hazelzet, H. (2006) Human rights aspects of EU crisis management operations, *International Peacekeeping*, 13(4), pp. 564–581.

Hill, C. (1993) The capability–expectations gap, or conceptualizing Europe's international role, *Journal of Common Market Studies*, 31(3), pp. 305–328.

Hill, C. (1998) Closing the capabilities–expectations gap?, in J. Peterson and H. Sjursen (Eds.), *A Common Foreign Policy for Europe?* New York: Routledge, pp. 19–41.

House of Lords (2011) *The EU and Sudan*, HL Paper 160. London: HMSO.

ICG (2005) *The EU/AU Partnership In Darfur*. Brussels: ICG.

ICG (2015) *Sudan and South Sudan's Merging Conflicts*. Brussels: ICG.

IRIN (2009) Sudan: NGO expulsion, http://www.irinnews.org/report/83370/sudan-ngo-expulsion-to-hit-darfurs-displaced, accessed 11 May 2015.

Jupille, J. and Caporaso, J.A. (1998) States, agency and rules, in C. Rhodes (Ed.), *The European Union in the World Community*. Lynne Rienner: Boulder, pp. 213–229.

Knight, W. A. (2000) *A Changing United Nations*. London: Palgrave.

Middleton, R., Melly, P. and Vines, A. (2011) *Implementing The EU Concept On Mediation*. Brussels: European Parliament.

Olsen, G. R. (2007), Between development policy and foreign policy ambitions., Paper prepared for EUSA 10th Biennial International Conference, Montreal, May.

Olsen, G. R. (2009) The EU and military conflict management in Africa, *International Peacekeeping*, 16(2), pp. 245–60.

Olsen, G. R. and Furness, M. (2014) Europeanization and the EU's comprehensive approach. Paper presented to Roskilde University, 23 November.

Patey, L. A. (Ed.) (2007) *Oil Development in Africa*. Copenhagen: DIIS.

Power, S. (2015) Remarks on peacekeeping, http://usun.state.gov/briefing/statements/238660.htm, accessed 17 May 2015.

Sicurelli, D. (2010) *The European Union's Africa Policies*. London: Ashgate.

Thomas, D. C. (2012) Still punching below its weight?, *Journal of Common Market Studies*, 50(3), pp. 457–474.

Toje, A. (2008) The consensus–expectations gap: explaining Europe's ineffective foreign policy, *Security Dialogue*, 39(1), pp. 121–141.

Vines, A. (2010) Rhetoric from Brussels and reality, *International Affairs*, 86(5), pp. 1091–1108.

Watkins, J. (2014) Aging influence: the Commonwealth in the 21st century, Harvard International Review, 36 (1), http://hir.harvard.edu/archives/7535, accessed 21 March 2015.

Williams, P. D. (2006) Military responses to mass killing, *International Peacekeeping*, 13(2), pp. 168–183.

Williams, P. D. and Bellamy, A. J. (2005) The responsibility to protect, *Security Dialogue*, 36(1), pp. 27–47.

Zwan, J. van der (2011) *Evaluating the EU's Role and Challenges in Sudan*. London: International Alert.

Opinion

The Commonwealth and Europe

STEVE CUTTS

I am writing this as we approach the 2015 general election in the UK, and it strikes me that there has probably never been as much focus on an intergovernmental organisation as there is currently in advance of this poll. Although, traditionally, elections have been fought around issues of more immediate impact to people's lives—such as tax, education, health and the economy (of course)—Europe is now very much at the forefront of many people's minds. This is one issue that starkly divides the various political parties, from the 'little Englanders' in UKIP and the Conservative Party who want out (and of the four countries that comprise the UK, it is only England that would vote to leave the European Union), to the more internationally enlightened parties of the centre and left who recognise that, whatever the flaws of the European Union (EU), the UK carries far more weight and has more influence as part of this geographic bloc than it ever would going it alone.

Conversely, the Commonwealth these days rarely registers more than a passing mention in the UK press, unless there is a story of corruption or a major happening in the Commonwealth Games (of course, at the Games in India in 2010, the press was treated to a story of corruption *and* the Commonwealth Games combined). Yet, five years ago, I think it is fair to say that one of the parties—the Conservatives—did have a genuine determination to revitalise the Commonwealth, recognising its potential as a soft power association with reach into some of the most dynamic markets in the world. The appointment of Lord David Howell, either a true visionary of what the Commonwealth should be, or a deluded romanticist about a fading post-colonial organisation depending on your point of view, showed that the new government was seeking to demonstrate its pro-Commonwealth credentials.

Bizarrely, certain figures in the Conservative-led Coalition government supported the Commonwealth because they perceived it in some way as an alternative to the EU, clinging to some prelapsarian mythical age, believing that Britain could restore the primacy of its trade with its former colonies and ignore the economic imperative of the EU. But it would not be fair to accuse Lord Howell—nor for that matter Foreign Secretary William Hague—of such arrant nonsense. They recognised the fundamental differences in the two associations.

THE COMMONWEALTH AND THE EUROPEAN UNION IN THE 21ST CENTURY

- The Commonwealth is a voluntary association of 53 member states comprising more than two billion citizens, which supports and promotes its common values of democracy and sustainable development, good governance, human rights, the rule of law, economic development, sustainable economic development, gender equality and youth. Its intergovernmental organisations, governed by heads of government, make decisions on the basis of consensus; unlike the EU, it has no qualified majority voting. The Commonwealth has a rich network of civil society organisations which keeps it closely in touch with public opinion on Commonwealth developments, but unlike the EU, it has no law-making power, or means of enforcing any of its agreements.
- The Commonwealth Secretariat is a co-ordinating body with specific mandates on behalf of the member governments but without a legal base governing their implementation. The political mandate of the Commonwealth is provided by the biennial Commonwealth Heads of Government Meeting. There is no founding and legally binding charter, unlike for most intergovernmental organisations, although I had the honour of leading and steering the drafting and negotiation process in the Secretariat that led to the signature by the Queen, the Head of the Commonwealth, of the Commonwealth Charter in 2013, which sets out the values of the association.
- Compared with the EU behemoth, the institutions of the Commonwealth have a tiny staffing complement and minuscule budgets for administering their programmes. Even the Secretariat, the largest of the Commonwealth institutions, has a staff complement of fewer than 300 (although the oft-cited 'fact' that this is fewer staff than in the United Nations canteen in New York is fallacious) and a total budget of less than £50m (or around 0.5% of the budget of the UK's Department for International Development).
- Unlike the EU, the Commonwealth Secretariat is not a development donor. However, its development arm, the Commonwealth Fund for Technical Co-operation (CFTC), does provide expert intellectual property and technical interventions based on the transfer of personnel from within its global membership.
- Of course, the EU is fundamentally different from the Commonwealth. It is a European Union of 28 sovereign governments. Because of its economic weight and genesis as a trading pact, it has gained huge global political, economic and trade negotiating influence. Its heads of government and ministers, in taking binding decisions on the basis of qualified majority voting in specific areas of policy, mandate their common institutions to implement these decisions with legally binding effect.

Though they are very different organisations and associations, the Commonwealth and the EU share many common values and common interests. Among them are democratic values, free trade, the recognition of the universality of respect for human rights and the role of women in all aspects of governance.

They are also linked in important ways. First, three of the EU's members are Commonwealth members, i.e. the UK, Malta and Cyprus. Second, two-thirds of Commonwealth countries make up just under half of the members of the ACP (African, Caribbean and Pacific) group with which the EU has a special relationship. Finally, the EU and the Commonwealth have based institutional collaboration on shared values in all the global and regional relations in which they participate, especially in the United Nations agencies and at the General Assembly.

THE COMMONWEALTH AND THE EUROPEAN UNION IN THE 21ST CENTURY

Politically, the Commonwealth has comparative advantages, which the EU should recognise and value in a partner. These derive from its influencing and convening powers and its common legacy of institutions, working methods, common language, and common administrative and legal processes. This has enormous benefits for sustaining cordial and mutually beneficial relationships among its membership. Indeed, the Commonwealth has developed a reputation among its members of being a 'trusted partner'. This can allow it to work with countries on very sensitive political issues, such as human rights and the running of democratic elections. It also offers a huge potential to play a significant international advocacy and global consensus-building role given that its membership comprises a microcosm of the world: rich, developing, large, small, island, landlocked.

The Commonwealth already works with the EU in an expanding number of areas—in countries that have experienced constitutional and political upheavals, in trade capacity building, in governance in Africa in collaboration with the African Union, in building consensus in global trade negotiations, in strengthening the Regional Economic Communities in Africa, the Caribbean and the Pacific, in human rights and many others fields. One especially effective area is a Commonwealth-conceived trade capacity-building programme, being taken forward in co-operation with the EU Commission and the ACP Secretariat as well as the Francophonie. This programme, dubbed Hub & Spokes, deploys young well-qualified policy personnel from the South to the offices of trade ministers in ACP countries. It is very highly regarded for the positive impact it is having.

However, given its diverse membership, spanning both hemispheres, representing a variety of sizes of countries and different stages of economic development, the Commonwealth is clearly not fulfilling its potential. It is representative of every region as well as regional and economic groupings. Its ability to build consensus, even within its diverse membership, should enable it to reach agreement of substantial global impact on current and important political, economic and social issues. As a vehicle for strengthening global co-operation, the Commonwealth should work better together with its strategic partners to advance good governance and sustainable economic development.

However, its annual budget for technical co-operation, administered through the CFTC, although ludicrously small compared with the billions of euros spent by the EU on development, is perhaps just sufficient to divert the Commonwealth into attempting projects on the ground instead of focusing on its comparative advantage of political consensus building, and leveraging its knowledge about governance and the rule of law, and its trusted partner status in many countries where other multilateral institutions suffer from historic mistrust.

New leadership is desperately needed to prevent the Commonwealth from fading into ever-deeper obscurity, and for it to be seen as anything more than an irrelevant historic relic from the age of colonialism. With its potential to reach across all the different international groupings, the G77 and China, the EU and the other 'like-minded' countries, it could be a genuine force for good, helping the international system to mature and be in a position to rise to the global challenges facing it. This year, Commonwealth heads of government will be faced with the choice of the new Secretary-General to lead the association. With strong leadership, the Commonwealth really could develop into a small, but key player in the international arena, helping to forge global agreements across the realms of good governance, human rights and sustainable development. Otherwise, its future will be dim: unlike the EU, if the Commonwealth did not exist, it

THE COMMONWEALTH AND THE EUROPEAN UNION IN THE 21ST CENTURY

is hard to imagine a great demand to create it. Yet the world would be robbed of one of the few bodies capable of oiling the wheels of the multilateral system so as to help it meet the huge global challenges it faces.

Opinion

CHOGM Returns to Malta: EU and Commonwealth Membership in the Mediterranean

GODFREY BALDACCHINO

The venue and timing of each Commonwealth Heads of Government Meeting (CHOGM) is bound to shape its character. CHOGM 2015 in Malta presents many unique opportunities for the Commonwealth. The obvious one is to elect a new Secretary-General to lead the organisation for the next four years. Another is for a CHOGM to take place (again) within the European Union (EU). (The Commonwealth heads of government met in Limassol, Cyprus, in 1993, but that country was not an EU member state at that time; and in Edinburgh in 1997.) The previous CHOGM within an EU member state was also in Malta, back in November 2005, with the island state having acceded to EU membership barely 18 months before.

Much has changed in Malta since hosting the previous CHOGM in 2005. The country has clearly usurped its former status as a post-colonial developing state and established itself as a thriving cosmopolitan jurisdiction. Having weathered the 2008 financial crisis fairly well, the country has been a refuge, and a new home, for various expatriates, including many from both EU and non-EU countries. The instability in North Africa, and particularly in Libya, 300 km away, is, however, of particular concern. A growing and more affluent population has generated worryingly high levels of private consumption (e.g. of private motor vehicles); but there are some notable initiatives in alternative energy use (photovoltaic solar panels in particular).

There is an interesting corollary between Malta's experience of Europeanisation and the opportunities presented by a CHOGM event on its shores. A tense national debate about the pros and cons of EU membership had preceded the country's eventual EU accession in 2004; after 11 years of membership, the concerns have shifted dramatically to specific policies, and particularly to how to manage the geopolitics associated with being very much at the edge of the EU. Malta is a small island state, with a land area of just over 315 km^2, located right at the fault line between the world's most populous and richest trading bloc to the north and a patchily unsettled region, with many potential emigrants looking for a better life, to the south. A humanitarian disaster has unfolded in that stretch of the Mediterranean sea where Malta is located, as human

THE COMMONWEALTH AND THE EUROPEAN UNION IN THE 21ST CENTURY

smugglers rake in profit from dispatching hopeful immigrants to Europe on vessels that may be unseaworthy: for so many hundreds of these, their journey of hope is a fatal one. Although not the main sources of European migration transiting via Malta, I would expect that the representatives of the 17 African countries members of the Commonwealth will be especially interested in reviewing the migration conundrum from the Malta and EU vantage points. This also goes for the candidate tipped to take over as Secretary-General of the Commonwealth in 2016: Botswana's Mmasekgoa Masire-Mwamba.

Another of Malta's key aspirations within the Commonwealth is to enrich the debate about the socio-economic and political challenges facing small (and often island) states. It is to the Commonwealth's credit that the very idea of a 'small state' as a focus of comparative research and policy analysis exists. Malta has a distinguished record in this field: so successful that, ironically, it (along with Cyprus, and outside the Commonwealth, Iceland) is not considered to be a small island developing state. Malta has pioneered some notable scholarship in a diverse range of issues that affect small states: such as climate change management, examination systems, adult education and economic vulnerability. Moreover, the University of Malta, my employer, is an institution of high repute: it is the oldest university in the Commonwealth outside Britain; it is firmly committed to support such ventures; and it boasts the necessary infrastructural and human resource capacity to ensure their success. In this vein, at the last CHOGM held in Sri Lanka, Malta's Prime Minister, Joseph Muscat, had announced his government's commitment to support the setting up of a Small States Centre of Excellence in Malta, also in acknowledgement of this leadership role. I would expect tangible progress on the setting up of this centre, and an agreement on its terms of reference, at the 2015 CHOGM.

The Malta 2015 CHOGM will also be the first to host a Women's Forum. This will raise awareness of women's issues in Commonwealth countries and show how women's contributions can have a positive impact politically, economically and socially. With the upbeat theme 'Women Ahead Be All that You Can Be', the forum will align with various other local, national and European initiatives that encourage gender mainstreaming and stronger participation by women in the formal labour market. Malta's participation rate among women aged between 25 and 30 years currently stands at around 75%, a rate that surpasses the EU average rate of 66%. Two out of every three students in university education in Malta is female.

The theme chosen for this year's CHOGM—Adding Global Value—speaks to the fundamental challenge facing the organisation. The Commonwealth's soft power, when and if properly applied and administered, can promote change, shame miscreants, embarrass misdemeanour and reward model behaviour. Such an unruffled diplomacy can affect the lives of 2.2 billion Commonwealth citizens, and more beyond, for the better. Proactive on the international stage, well-represented in most global institutions and an acknowledged leader in developing educational programmes around the world, the Commonwealth is an ideal channel, with the necessary resources, to *add global value*. Performing such a role is the very *raison d'être* of the Commonwealth: the regular soul-searching exercises about whether there is yet life in this august organisation in the 21st century would not materialise with such stridency, or would not be contemplated at all, were such an agenda rigorously and scrupulously pursued. CHOGM in Malta in 2015 should provide a timely opportunity for sober reflection, and apposite action.

Opinion

Back to the Future: The EU and the Commonwealth

CARL WRIGHT

Forty years ago—in 1975—British people voted in a referendum to stay in what was then the European Community (EC). Now, in 2015, the UK is on the verge of another referendum on whether to remain a member of the European Union (EU). Then, the impact of Britain's relationship with the Commonwealth was an issue. Now, certainly in the recent UK election, the question of the Commonwealth as an alternative to EU membership has been raised, notably by the nationalist UKIP party of Nigel Farage.

On 1 January 1975, Britain became a member of the EC and the following day I was one of the first 10 or so UK nationals to start to work in the European Commission in the office of George Thomson, who had also been a minister for the Commonwealth. After Brussels, I took on a job with a Commonwealth organisation in 1980 and have stayed working within different Commonwealth bodies, including the Commonwealth Secretariat, for the last 35 years.

Does this mean that I now wish to substitute the Commonwealth for the EU? Not at all—only in January this year I was with the European Commissioner for Development, signing a seven-year partnership agreement with my organisation, the Commonwealth Local Government Forum (CLGF). This provides funding supplementary to that derived from the Department for International Development and other Commonwealth sources and opens up significant EU funds for our work to promote local democracy and good governance, including in Zimbabwe where we recently secured a €1 million EU contract. Indeed, we have bid for, and won, EU project grants for 20 years, which have all directly benefited our Commonwealth members.

Does this imply being seduced by Brussels 'gold'? Not in the least—EU contracts have tough reporting and accounting conditions, require substantial co-funding from other sources and need to be results-orientated. Securing these is no different from securing grants from other development partners and, in any case, much EU funding is derived from the taxpayers of the UK, as well as Cyprus and Malta, which are also EU members.

Money, although important, is not everything. More significant is the ability to influence EU policy-making. Thus, in 2013 I flew to Dublin to meet the Irish development minister, who was the president of the European Council dealing with an

THE COMMONWEALTH AND THE EUROPEAN UNION IN THE 21ST CENTURY

important EU Communication on Local Authorities in development policy. On account of this, and through lobbying by our European partners in the PLATFORMA network, with whom CLGF shares a collective office in Brussels, the Communication was successfully adopted. As result there is greater recognition for local government's role in development throughout the Commonwealth, more access to EU funds by our members and political spin-offs in the current negotiations in New York designed to ensure that the new United Nations post-2015 development agenda is implemented bottom-up, not top-down.

So what does all this mean for the bigger picture and the imminent UK referendum on Europe? There is clearly much for Commonwealth countries to gain by Britain staying an active member of the EU; by being able to influence EU policy which has a direct bearing on them, whether in the field of development or trade and investment; and by maintaining access to significant EU development, regional and social funds.

I can think of no Commonwealth country that wants Britain to leave the EU. Over the past year or so, I have met Commonwealth leaders from Ghana, Jamaica, Malta, Papua New Guinea, Rwanda, Sri Lanka, Tuvalu and Uganda, and ministers and local government leaders from many others. I cannot think of a single one who wants to see 'Brexit' from the EU; indeed, most are horrified by the prospect!

What then is the way to the future for the EU and the Commonwealth, as opposed to a return to the past? In many ways, the EU is too big and bureaucratic, while the Commonwealth is too small—at least in resources—and too informal: the EU is notorious for institutional complexity and red tape, while the Commonwealth is too fragmented and insufficiently joined-up among its 70-plus diverse organisations. The EU struggles with deploying its massive development funds, while the Commonwealth is starved of funds.

There is therefore a strong case for the two organisations benefiting from each other's comparative advantages; not seeing each as in competition or as alternatives. It is, however, not just UK anti-Europeans who should to go to Specsavers for the right glasses to read the fine print of EU–Commonwealth relations. Many Europeans wrongly see the Commonwealth as an offshoot of the British Empire, while they have no problems about Brussels happily giving support—and money—to La Francophonie, arguably much closer to French interests: all need to recognise the remarkable outreach, networks and political legitimacy of the Commonwealth of 53 proudly independent Commonwealth countries.

Clearly, there is scope for the EU and the Commonwealth to work together, perhaps by having a Commonwealth organisations' office in Brussels. In this endeavour, the UK should link up strategically with Cyprus and Malta and like-minded countries such as Ireland: for example, in 2017, when Prime Minister Muscat of Malta will hold both the EU presidency and the chair of the Commonwealth. Any 'renegotiation' of EU terms by David Cameron should therefore also take the Commonwealth dimension into account.

I spend much time in Kent, close to the Channel Tunnel, where every day innumerable lorries, cars and tourists arrive as a testimony of the UK's close commercial links with Europe. 'Brexit' would inflict huge damage on the UK economy; it would equally do a grave disservice to our Commonwealth partners. Ironically, Thanet in East Kent, although it rejected Mr Farage at the UK parliamentary elections, has the only UKIP local council in Britain. Given that Thanet itself benefits from EU grants,

THE COMMONWEALTH AND THE EUROPEAN UNION IN THE 21ST CENTURY

voting for Brexit there is like turkeys voting for Christmas. However, do not expect our Commonwealth partners to support a UK exit from Europe: they realise that British membership of the EU and of the Commonwealth are both essential and indeed are complementary to each other, and that they are not in any way alternative options.

Opinion

Singapore and Europe: From Strength to Strength

CLAIRE SANDERSON

On 9 August 2015, Singapore celebrates 50 years of independence and a remarkable success story against the odds. In half a century, the tiny city-state has become a prosperous economic and strategic pivot, a leading power in the region and a legitimate player on the international stage. Singapore's relations with Europe have played, and continue to play, a relevant part in this process, while contributing to the increasing importance given to inter-regional dialogue on the international stage.

For at least the first 30 years, Singapore's political, social and economic transformation owed much to the vision and determination of its Prime Minister Lee Kuan Yew, whose successful though often controversial policies led the 'red dot' from strength to strength. A regional and global thinker, Lee understood that Singapore's survival depended on its unique position not just within South-East Asia, but globally. A member of the United Nations and the Commonwealth since 1965, Singapore became one of the founder members of the Association of South-East Asian Nations (ASEAN) in 1967, where it would play an important role in the diplomatic, economic and institutional rapprochement between South-East Asia and Europe.

Singapore's relationship with the evolving European bloc was an integral part of Lee's vision of the future, and he did not want Singapore to be excluded from this potentially huge economic market. He cultivated personal relations with successive European leaders, France and Germany especially, and between 1972 and 1978 Singapore signed a series of bilateral investment treaties with the Netherlands, Germany, France, the UK, Switzerland, and the Belgium–Luxemburg Economic Union. In the meantime, the European Economic Community (EEC) in 1992 had adopted a policy of inter-regional dialogue and rapprochement with ASEAN as a whole, laying the foundations for future cooperation. South-East Asia and Europe began to look to each other: the first Europe–ASEAN ministerial meeting was held in 1978, and in 1980 the EEC–ASEAN Cooperation Agreement set up a Joint Cooperation Committee, introducing an institutional dimension to these inter-regional relations for the first time.

During the years that followed, and as the international climate evolved, Singapore and ASEAN witnessed the development of the European Single Market, the North American Free Trade Area, the emerging economies in Eastern Europe as the Cold War

THE COMMONWEALTH AND THE EUROPEAN UNION IN THE 21ST CENTURY

came to an end, and the evolution of the EEC, now the European Union (EU). The ASEAN response was to create its own Free Trade Area, in 1992, to stimulate intra-regional competition and its own economies. But the rapprochement between Europe and South-East Asia continued nonetheless, and was given new momentum in 1996 at the first Asia Europe Meeting (ASEM) summit in Bangkok. A Franco-Singapore initiative, ASEM brought together 25 foreign ministers from ASEAN, the EU, China, Japan and South Korea for inter-regional dialogue on political, economic and socio-cultural issues. It was followed a year later by the first ASEM Foreign Ministers' Meeting establishing the first ASEM institution, the Asia–Europe Foundation, an intergovernmental platform for cultural dialogue and exchange located in Singapore.

As Singapore continued its spectacular growth, becoming one of the four Asian Tigers and a significant regional player with international recognition, the EU came to embrace Singapore as a partner in its own right. The EU was already strengthening relations with individual ASEAN countries through Partnership and Cooperation Agreements, but Singapore was the first ASEAN country to sign a free trade agreement as an individual country. The EU–Singapore Free Trade Agreement (EUSFTA) came into force in 2014, replacing the existing bilateral investment treaties between Singapore and EU members. It represented a significant achievement for the city-state, and complemented the free trade agreements already in force with the majority of its non-European trading partners. It was largely welcomed by the EU as well, not only for economic reasons, but also to help raise EU visibility in South-East Asia, a process that began in 2009 with the establishment of a European Union Centre in Singapore.

For the EU today, Singapore represents a gateway to the Asia-Pacific and a bridge between the markets and institutions of these two giant regions. The EUSFTA of 2014 also opened the door for free trade agreements between the EU and other ASEAN members, whose expanding markets and regional and consumer growth are seen as potentially beneficial to European exports, investment and employment. The EU today is Singapore's third trade partner (more than €46 billion in 2014), its top investor and its top supplier. Although Singapore is only the EU's 15th trade partner overall, it remains important and is its biggest ASEAN trade partner. In 2014, more than 10,000 European companies were operating in Singapore; start-ups are supported by the France–Singapore Business Council, the UK–ASEAN Business Council, the German Centre for Industry and Trade and German–Singapore Chamber of Industry and Commerce, the Russia–Singapore Business Forum, and the Nordic European Centre, for example. Agreements such as the Enhanced Partnerships with Germany and Switzerland, the Singapore–France Joint Declaration on Strategic Partnership, and the High-level Inter-Russia–Singapore Governmental Commission all contribute to this dynamic. ASEM today counts 53 members, representing almost half of the world's gross domestic product, 60% of its population, and 60% of global trade; its remit extends to issues of regional and international concern.

Of course, Singapore's relations with Europe are not limited to the EU and its member states. Singapore has also developed economic relations with Central and Eastern Europe and other regions; it opened an embassy in Turkey in 2012; and in 2013 Singapore joined the Arctic Council as an observer, strengthening relations with Norway, Denmark, Sweden, Finland, Russia and Iceland. Nor are relations between Singapore and Europe defined in only economic terms, although these have overtaken defence and strategic considerations over the years. Cooperation exists and thrives in many other domains: science, technology, education, research and development, energy, climate change, to name but a few. Cooperation in culture and the arts, the Alliance Française, the British Council, the Goethe-Institut and the Italian Cultural Institute all contribute to the considerable investment in culture and the arts in Singapore today.

Strengthened by the consequences of economic growth and cooperation, the many dimensions of relations between Singapore and Europe continue to deepen and flourish, a credit to the legacy of Lee Kuan Yew. Inter-regional dialogue has gained considerable weight on the international stage, and the ASEM initiatives have added an institutional dimension to inter-regional cooperation. Sadly, Lee did not live to celebrate Singapore's 50th anniversary of independence. The extraordinary tributes by Singaporeans and on the streets of Singapore during the week of national mourning that followed his death on 23 March 2015, from friends and foes alike, were a poignant and immensely moving homage to the vision and achievements of an extraordinary, if controversial, individual. Today, Singapore's relations with Europe continue to grow, and both Singapore and Europe look to benefit from investing in these relations in the future.

Opinion

Understanding Student Mobility: An Agenda for EU/Commonwealth Discussion

JOHN KIRKLAND

Student mobility should be an ideal area for collaboration between Europe and the Commonwealth. There is broad consensus that higher education should become international. There is recognition that the time that we spend as students has a disproportionate influence on shaping our future attitudes. After two decades of tragic neglect by the international development community, higher education is once again seen as critical to economic and social development. The interests of developing and developed countries —though not common—would seem to have strong synergy. The former need to expand their qualified labour force at a rate that domestic supply cannot meet; the latter need to attract international talent to maintain the quality, reputation and—all too often —financial stability of their own universities.

Mobility remains largely market led. It has expanded in an unplanned manner. Even where financed by donors, mobility tends to be ad hoc and lacking international strategic direction and common vision—even more than one would expect given the different priorities and emphasis that naturally occur between donors. New schemes are produced with regularity, but often display a depressing tendency to reinvent the wheel. International programmes for student mobility tend to look very different from the perspectives of developing and developed country participants.

Discussions between European and Commonwealth programmes—as with most donors—are rare. If they did take place, what would they focus on? Here I suggest a five-point agenda that could be developed to put mobility into a global context.

First, what *are* the benefits of mobility, and what is the relationship between them? A wide range of potential benefits is suggested—from the development of specific skills to the wider development of 'international peace and understanding'—but some are ill-defined, and we know too little about student motivations. Rectifying this could have an important impact on policy. It will help to predict whether the development of stronger universities in developing countries is a prerequisite to greater mobility, or a threat to it, and how far the increased availability of MOOCs (massive open online courses) and other distance learning methods will be seen as an alternative to full-scale mobility.

THE COMMONWEALTH AND THE EUROPEAN UNION IN THE 21ST CENTURY

Second, how do we know whether these benefits have been achieved? Governments and other donors increasingly require evidence that their investments have an impact. Scholarships and other mobility schemes have not been good at providing this, beyond initial opinion surveys. Nor are there agreed methodologies for doing so. In recent years bodies such as the Commonwealth Scholarships Commission in the United Kingdom have been seeking to rectify this, but the field is well suited to international collaboration.

Third, how can we ensure that mobility is *genuinely* international, rather than being primarily south to north. Some encouraging trends exist. The number of exchange and short-term students going to developing countries has risen markedly. This is a step in the right direction—and should be seen as such. If we really view mobility as a route to international understanding many more need actually to study for qualifications in developing countries—and host universities need to be able to accommodate them. There is also scope for further expansion in south-to-south mobility schemes.

Fourth, what is the relationship between self-financing and sponsored mobility? Does the latter encourage the former? Do sponsored students have specific characteristics— in terms of ability or social background, for example? How far do they have an impact on wider mobility—or a disproportionate impact on capacity building? Given the huge numbers of self-financing international students, these are important issues in justifying why donors invest in mobility at all. For universities that offer scholarships, too, it is important to know how their awards affect the demand from fee-paying students. At best, they could act as loss-leaders that bring the institution to the attention of a wider market. At worst, they do not increase the market at all, and simply make places available to those who would otherwise have paid for them.

Finally, if expanding mobility *is* important, how will it be financed? On the assumption that scholarships will be limited, does the growth of mobility depend on a growing middle class that is willing and able to pay for it? Can alternative incentives be found —or is the cost of mobility simply added to the rising costs of higher education as a whole? If we rely on the latter, and if mobility is seen as an asset in the labour market, then what equity issues emerge?

People make too many assumptions about mobility and its capacity to expand. It is on this basis that universities in many developed countries have allowed their finances to depend so heavily on overseas students. Pursuing this agenda should not be seen as questioning this importance. Quite the reverse—it is so important that the forces underlying it need to be understood properly. The shock waves generated by relatively small declines in overseas student numbers in some developed countries in recent years, after two decades of growth, provide a warning of the impact if we get our assumptions wrong.

Opinion

Why and How Should the Commonwealth of Nations Engage in the Access and Benefit-sharing Issue

AMANDINE ORSINI

The Nagoya Protocol on Access to Genetic Resources and the Fair and Equitable Sharing of Benefits Arising from their Utilisation (hereafter Nagoya Protocol), adopted in 2010 during the 10th Conference of the Parties to the Convention on Biological Diversity, entered into force in October 2014. The idea behind the protocol is that biodiversity, and more precisely the genetic resources of plants and animals, is useful for a number of commercial applications, including pharmaceutical, cosmetic and agricultural. As a result, the protocol proposes a legal basis asking the users of genetic resources to share part of their commercial profits with the providers of these resources. Sometimes, users also take inspiration from traditional knowledge to develop their commercial applications. The protocol therefore applies to genetic resources and to the associated traditional knowledge.

The Commonwealth of Nations cannot be considered as an active multilateral association in global environmental politics. As early as 1989 the Commonwealth Heads of Government Meeting adopted the Langkawi Declaration on the Environment. Yet, 25 years later, the Commonwealth Secretariat announced on its website its political engagement for only two environmental issues: climate change and rapid urbanisation. These topics were added to its agenda owing to the real threat they pose to several of its members. In particular, small island states are highly vulnerable to a potential sea-level rise and developing countries face issues of urban overpopulation and poverty.

While the Commonwealth has been reactive so far, there is room for it to embrace proactively certain environmental problems. Engaging in new issues, such as the recent access and benefit-sharing one (ABS issue), would be beneficial for the intergovernmental body in terms of economic benefits and reputational gains.

Such an engagement would not require exaggerated efforts. Overall, 19 Commonwealth members have already ratified the Nagoya Protocol: 16 individually and three under the banner of the European Union. Despite its general label as 'environmental', the ABS issue stands at the crossroads of at least three other key international concerns: economic gains, development and the recognition of indigenous peoples. While several

THE COMMONWEALTH AND THE EUROPEAN UNION IN THE 21ST CENTURY

Commonwealth countries are already active on these aspects of the ABS issue individually, the uniqueness of its membership may provide the Commonwealth with the potential to embrace collectively the role of a leader.

Encouraging industrial sectors such as forestry and fisheries is already on the agenda of the Commonwealth. The sectors using genetic resources could be added to the list of economic activities to be encouraged by the organisation. Several Commonwealth states, such as the United Kingdom and Australia, are important users of genetic resources, in particular for biotechnology applications. Conversely, several Commonwealth states are providers of genetic resources. This is particularly the case for Malaysia, South Africa, Kenya and India, members of the Group of Like-minded Megadiverse Countries, a coalition gathering 15 countries owning more than 70% of the world's biodiversity. On the part of users, adopting the protocol could bring certainty in international exchanges of genetic resources. On the part of providers, it would help countries put an end to biopiracy cases, whereby genetic resources are exploited without compensation. The cases of the Hoodia cactus in South Africa or of Basmati rice in India are renowned cases of biopiracy, involving the misappropriation of indigenous knowledge.

The generated economic benefits could be reinvested to solve some of the development problems of several Commonwealth states. The ABS issue is closely linked to development, particularly for poor countries that rely heavily on natural resources for their livelihoods. Moreover, within these countries, it is mostly local actors who will benefit from ABS measures.

Development in the ABS context is closely related to the status of indigenous and local populations who use and develop knowledge on genetic resources. In December 2007, the United Nations General Assembly adopted the Declaration on the Rights of Indigenous Peoples. This declaration came at a time when the Commonwealth risked attracting criticism, with one reason being the poor performance of its member states in acknowledging and promoting the human rights of indigenous peoples located in their territories. Countries such as Canada, Australia and New Zealand even acted collectively to try to prevent the adoption of the declaration. Moreover, several African states, members of the Commonwealth, actively delayed the adoption of the declaration for almost a year. The Commonwealth should anticipate reputational problems related to indigenous rights. Anticipating these problems can be done through the ABS issue. While some Commonwealth members have sometimes been laggards on indigenous issues, others, such as India, have proposed innovative solutions to protect indigenous knowledge, such as the creation of official registers and databases.

Finally, engaging in the ABS treaty would confirm the commitment of Commonwealth states to environmental protection. Investing in the use of genetic resources is equivalent to granting them an economic value and therefore creating the incentive to protect them *in situ*. According to the Nagoya Protocol, the benefits generated by the compensation for access to genetic resources could be reinvested in biodiversity conservation.

More than the economic benefits to be drawn from a clear framework for the use of genetic resources, being engaged in the ABS issue could bring several reputational benefits to the Commonwealth of Nations. It would demonstrate that the organisation engages in topical environmental issues, is concerned by indigenous rights, and is able to go beyond a traditional north/south divide. Indeed, a rather strong north/south divide

THE COMMONWEALTH AND THE EUROPEAN UNION IN THE 21ST CENTURY

animates the ABS issue because countries rich in biodiversity are mostly developing countries, while countries skilled at using genetic resources are mostly developed countries. The Commonwealth of Nations would show that it is possible to overcome such differences, embracing the positive role of 'leader by example'.

One solution would be for the Commonwealth to produce a collective position in favour of the adoption of the Nagoya Protocol by all its members. To facilitate the implementation of the agreement, the organisation could also take inspiration from the European Union, which adopted a special Regulation on ABS—Regulation (EU) No. 511/2014—in April 2014. This regulation does not impose a unique law for all European member states but establishes a common framework and minimum requirements for the harmonisation of future national legislations on the issue.

Index

access and benefit-sharing (ABS) issue 115–17
Anyaoku, Emeka 34, 35
Ashton, Catherine 90

Bashir, Omar al 89–94, 96
Bin Laden, Osama 73
bipolar perspectives 15, 30–1, 34
Blair, Tony 88, 95
Boko Haram 32
branding 35
Brylle, Torben 89, 91, 94

Cameron, David 95, 108
'capabilities–expectations model' 85–7, 98
Caribbean: Europe and 42–51; free trade
    agreements with 45; Lomé Conventions and
    43–4, 47–9; preference levels for 45; trade
    protocols for 42–4
challenges: for humanitarianism 70–2; for India
    70–83; normative challenges 14–25; structural
    challenges 14–15
Chirac, Jacques 95
'civil paths' 34, 36
Clarkson, Adrienne 36
codes of conduct 3, 13
commercial diplomacy 7
Commonwealth: access and benefit-sharing
    issue 115–17; 'Brexit' and 108–9; broader
    perspectives on 50–1; comparisons of 1–3,
    11–24, 101–3; cooperation of 6–8; cross-
    perspectives on 54–65; development aid
    and 17–21; dialogue for 6–8; diplomatic
    networks of 7; Europe and 101–4; European
    Union and 107–9; foreign policy and
    12–14; foreign relations and 32; future of
    1, 107–9; global crisis and 27–39; global
    development and 27–39; humanitarian
    assistance 56–65; humanitarian concerns
    59–65; humanitarianism and 54–65; image
    of 7; improving relations 7–8; innovations of
    11–12, 28, 34–8, 64, 70–1, 116; international
    organisations and 54–65; inter-state
    membership of 28–38; moral agenda of 12–14;

moral persuasions 21–3; normative challenges
    14–15; normative conditions 4–5; normative
    persuasions 21–3; opportunities offered by 8;
    partnerships and 1–8; perspectives on 28–9;
    roles of 1–3; soft power and 6, 11–25; strategic
    dialogue with 8; structural challenges 14–15;
    student mobility and 113–14; 'transnational'
    perspectives on 28–9
Commonwealth Caribbean: broader perspectives
    on 50–1; Europe and 42–51; free trade
    agreements and 45; Lomé Conventions and
    43–4, 47–9; preference levels for 45; trade
    protocols for 42–4
Commonwealth Games 28, 31, 35–6, 80, 101
Commonwealth Heads of Government Meeting
    (CHOGM) 1, 32–3, 54–5, 105–6
conflict management 7, 85–98
conflict resolution 7, 32–3, 37–8, 63, 81, 85–98
Cotonou Agreement 47–8

Darfur Crisis 85–98; see also Sudan
decolonisation 3, 35, 58
development aid 15–21
development–humanitarian divide 62–5
development policy changes 45–6
diasporas 28–39
disaster management 54–9, 63–5
disaster preparedness 63–5
'disaster relief industry' 71
disaster risk reduction programmes 54–9, 63–5
Dunant, Henri 72–3

'emerging markets' 29–32; see also markets
Europe: Caribbean and 42–51; Commonwealth
    and 101–4; Singapore and 110–12
European Economic Community (EEC) 2–6,
    43–9, 59, 63, 110–11
European Union (EU): 'Brexit' and 108–9;
    broader perspectives on 50–1; Commonwealth
    and 107–9; comparisons of 1–3, 11–24,
    101–3; as conflict manager 7, 85–98;
    cooperation of 6–8; cross-perspectives
    on 54–65; development aid and 15–17;

INDEX

development policies of 5; development policy changes 45–6; dialogue for 6–8; diplomatic networks of 7; enlargement of 46; 'fitness for purpose' and 86–7, 91–4; foreign policy and 12–14; free trade agreements 45; future of 1, 85–98, 107–9; global crisis and 27–39; global development and 27–39; humanitarian assistance 56–65; humanitarian concerns 59–65; humanitarianism and 54–65; image of 7; improving relations 7–8; innovations of 11–12; instruments of 92–3; international organisations and 54–65; Lomé Conventions and 43–4, 47–9; moral agenda of 12–14; moral persuasions 21–3; normative challenges 14–15; normative conditions 4–5; normative persuasions 21–3; opportunities offered by 8; overseas territories and 49–50; partnerships and 1–8; power of 4–5; resources of 91–3; roles of 1–3, 33; soft power and 11–25; strategic dialogue with 8; structural challenges 14–15; student mobility and 113–14; tools of 92–3; trade protocols 42–4; unity of 93–4

Farage, Nigel 107, 108
'fitness for purpose' 86–7, 91–4
foreign assistance 62–5, 74
foreign policy: Commonwealth and 12–14; European Union and 12–14; soft power and 12–14
foreign relations 32; *see also* international relations
free trade agreements (FTAs) 20, 42, 45, 48, 111
'frontier markets' 31–2; *see also* markets
functionalism 5–6

Geneva Convention 57–8, 73
genocide 58, 62, 74, 85, 88, 95, 98
global crisis 27–39
global development 27–39
global security 34–5
global trade rules 4, 44
government–civil society relations 7–8

Haavisto, Pekko 89, 91
Hagglund, Gustav 88
Hague, William 101
Heyzer, Noeleen 36
'house values' 11–12, 21–3
Howell, Lord David 20, 24, 101
human development: international relations and 27, 31–4; security and 29, 33–9
humanitarian assistance: Commonwealth and 6, 56–65; European Union and 56–65; India and 72–9; international relations and 54–5

humanitarian concerns: Commonwealth and 59–65; European Union and 59–65; South Africa and 59–64
humanitarian–development divide 62–5
humanitarianism: challenges for 70–2; Commonwealth and 54–65; European Union and 54–65; evolution of 54–65; in India 70–83
humanitarian programmes 55–65, 72–80
humanitarian regime 70–83
humanitarian rhetoric 75–8
humanitarian system 55–6, 81–3
human rights 2–6, 35
human security 29, 33–9

immigration concerns 29, 59
India: challenge of 70–83; 'emergence' of 71; as humanitarian actor 72, 74–5, 82; humanitarian practices in 78–81; humanitarian regime in 70–83; humanitarian rhetoric of 75–8; soft power and 76, 80
innovations 11–12, 28, 34–8, 64, 70–1, 116
international development 37
international diplomacy 7; *see also* international relations
international humanitarian regime 72–4
international organisations 54–65; *see also* international relations
international politics 5–7, 30, 71, 74, 78
international relations: bipolar perspectives of 30–1, 34; coalitions and 24; conception of 2; fairness of 5–6; human development and 27, 31–4; humanitarian assistance and 54–5; international development and 37; normative power and 2, 5–6; regulation of 5; studies of 11–14; transformation of 2–3; 'transnational' perspectives of 29–37
inter-regional diplomacy 4, 7

Jagdeo, Bharrat 48

Kiir, Salva 90

Lee Kuan Yew 110, 112
Lomé Conventions 3, 43–4, 47–9

Machar, Riek 90
Malta 1, 54–5, 105–6
Mansingh, Lalit 79
markets: 'emerging markets' 29–32; 'frontier markets' 31–2; regional markets 47–8; weakening of 29
Marsden, Rosalind 89, 91
Masire-Mwamba, Mmasekgoa 22, 106
Mathai, Wangiri 36

INDEX

Mcfee, Deborah 38
migration concerns 7, 29–31, 34–5, 38, 59, 106
mobility: agenda for 113–14; Commonwealth and 113; European Union and 113
Modi, Narendra 76–80
moral agenda 12–14
moral persuasions 21–3
multilateralism 6, 11–12, 28, 35–8
Muscat, Joseph 106, 108
Mutota, Folade 38

Nagoya Protocol 115–17
'norm–aid disconnect' 18–24
normative challenges: Commonwealth and 14–15; development aid and 15–16; European Union and 14–15; 'norm–aid disconnect' 18–24; qualitative effect of 15–16; soft power and 14–25; structural challenges and 14–15
normative disconnect 22; *see also* 'norm–aid disconnect'
normative persuasions 21–3
normative power: fragmentation and 15; international relations and 2, 5–6; soft power and 5–6, 12–14
'norm–norm disconnect' 24
norms: democratic norms 30–6; in post-colonial era 2–4; recasting 2–4; setting 4–8
North–South Peace Process 85–6, 89–95

Obama, Barack 78
overseas territories 49–50

partnerships 1–8; *see also* international relationships
peace-building 7, 32–3, 37–8, 90
peace-making 7, 85–95
policies: adjusting 4–8; development policy changes 45–6; foreign policy 12–14; formulation of 3; impact of 17; range of 13
Powell, Colin 88

Ramphal, Sonny 34, 35
Ramphele, Mamphele 36
refugee crisis 62, 78–80
refugee protection 71, 74, 80

regional markets 47–8; *see also* markets
Rylander, Sten 89

security 29, 33–9
Sen, Amartya 34, 36
Sen, Nirupam 77
Sharma, Kamalesh 38, 80
Singapore 110–12
Singh, Manmohan 76
soft power: Commonwealth and 6, 11–25; defining 12–13; European Union and 11–25; foreign policy and 12–14; India and 76, 80; moral agenda and 12–13; normative challenges and 14–25; normative power and 5–6, 12–14; Sudan and 91, 95
South Africa 59–64
Straw, Jack 88
structural challenges 14–15
student mobility: agenda for 113–14; Commonwealth and 113; European Union and 113
Sudan: conflict management in 85–98; Darfur Crisis in 85–98; disunity and 93–4; European Union and 85–98; 'fitness for purpose' and 86–7, 91–4; human resources for 91; instruments for 92–3; North–South Peace Process 85–6, 89–95; peace-making in 85–95; political space in 90, 96–8; resources for 91–3; soft power and 91, 95; strategies for 91–7; target setting for 95–7; tools for 92–3; unity for 93–4

terrorist attacks 34–5
terrorist groups 32; *see also* al-Qaeda; Boko Haram
Thomson, George 107
trade protocols 42–4
trade rules 4, 44
'transnational' perspectives 28–37

United Kingdom: European Union and 1; overseas territories and 49–50

Wilson, Harold 60

Yaoundé Conventions 3, 43, 49, 63